HOW TO NOT SUCK™ AT CYBERSECURITY

Vincent C. Romney

CISSP. CCSP. CSSLP

HOWTONOTSUCK

eBook ISBN: 978-1-968711-00-9

Print ISBN: 978-1-968711-01-6

Audiobook: 978-1-968711-02-3

Printed in the United States of America

Publisher: Vincent C Romney

Book design and layout: Vincent C Romney & Elaine Canyon

About the How To Not Suck Series

Live better. Suck less.

A message from Deirdre F. Gallagher, Founder of the How to Not Suck Movement:

On the journey to get better at the stuff life throws at us—money, leadership, relationships, neurodivergent brains, you name it—I realized something: most of us are walking around thinking we're the only ones who suck at basic things. Well, we're not.

The HOW TO NOT SUCK series was born from a moment of clarity that hit me after being diagnosed with ADHD as an adult. It explained why although I had an "outwardly successful life" (with achievements like a Wharton MBA, career wins, and raising 3 great kids) I was still struggling in several areas. What started as my own search for tools and frameworks quickly became the seed for a movement—one grounded in honesty, humor, and a deep belief that we're not meant to figure this out alone. I arrived at what I call the AWAKEN Framework—Awareness, Wellness, Action, Knowledge, Emotions, and Networking—and it guides the entire series, giving structure to the chaos of self-improvement.

Every book in this series tackles a topic we all wish we were better at—but often feel too overwhelmed (or too ashamed) to admit we need help with. Written by real experts and vetted by other domain pros, these aren't just "inspirational reads." They're practical, tough-love field guides for getting out of the rut and into real progress.

No fake gurus. No fluff. Just better tools, fewer faceplants, and a little more grace as we figure it out together.

Because life's too short to suck at the stuff that matters. Find more at www.howtonotsuck.com

Dedication

First, to my wife and kids, who have borne the brunt of the impact of both my military and civilian careers in IT and cybersecurity. There's nothing easy about the uncertainty and separation, and you have had to "figure it out" while I was out doing my job. You are all amazing human beings and I love you!

Second, to my colleagues and associates in Cyber. I learn from you every day, and we are all better together. I could not do what I do without the influence you've provided, and continue to provide.

Lastly, to the defenders in every home, small business, and boardroom. You didn't sign up for a cyber war, but you're in one. Stay strong. Stay sharp. Stay snarky.

Table of Contents

Foreword

Because No One Else Wrote the Damn Thing

Let's start with a confession.

This book was born out of irritation... Frustration... Maybe even full-blown security-nerd rage.

I kept coming across cybersecurity books that promised to be "for small businesses", "entrepreneurs", etc... You know, supposedly "accessible for non-technical audiences", and meant to help them navigate their cybersecurity journey.

Spoiler alert: they weren't.

They were 400 pages that restated every known regulatory code and security framework, filled with buzzwords wrapped in spreadsheets and diagrams, written by someone who probably hasn't touched a router since the Bush administration (pick one). Or worse, whose technical proficiency is bar-none, but has great difficulty speaking full sentences without a dozen acronyms. Some chapters were basically just a remix of ***NIST*** 800-53—with a motivational quote slapped on top and a stock photo of a lock. (For context, NIST 800-53 is a collection of security controls focused on the Government sector that reads like stereo instructions from 1974).

And I thought: *Are you kidding me, who can take anything away from this other than discouragement?*

We're drowning in bad advice. Or worse, advice that's technically accurate but completely unusable unless you've got a full-time IT staff to interpret it, a 7-figure security budget, and a team of auditors living in your break room.

So I wrote this.

A guide for real people. Living in the real world. Running real businesses. Using real devices that get real malware. **And it's short**. It's a book you can read in an evening... and keep as a reference for the next decade.

I use stories from various sources to illustrate the concepts to be covered in each chapter. Some of these are things I personally experienced in military exercises or operations, and are redacted sufficiently to avoid any exposure of classified information. Some are experiences I or my colleagues have experienced in the enterprise environment, and are likewise changed to avoid any identification to their organizations. Others are taken from events reported in the news, and are therefore stated "as is", because if something hits the news, we better all learn from it.

This book isn't for cybersecurity professionals (although they'll hopefully nod along and mutter "finally" while reading it). And hey, if you read something you don't understand, there's a glossary at the back (most, if not all, glossary items will be in bold italic so you'll know). There's also Google...

The Four Personas (aka Who This Book Is For)

We're going to break this down into four human types—because no matter how big or small your digital footprint, you're in one, two, or even all of these camps:

1. **The Individual**: The regular human. You have email. A

smartphone. Social media. And probably no clue what your router's password is. Or that it has firmware. Or that it *needs* updates.

2. **The Side-Hustler**: You run a Shopify store. You sell handmade ***crypto***-pinecones on Etsy. You have a Facebook page and maybe even a domain name.

3. **The Mid-Cap Boss**: You've got employees. A real business. Maybe even some outsourced IT. But cybersecurity? Not really baked into the cake.

4. **The Enterprise Executive**: You sit on top of a billion-dollar castle built on code, contracts, and compliance nightmares. You have a security team. You just need to actually listen to them... and guide them to give you useful metrics.

Each chapter walks through a core security principle, aligned with the ***Center for Internet Security (CIS) Top 18 Controls*** (https://www.cisecurity.org/controls/cis-controls-list), but translated into something useful. Practical. Sometimes blunt. Occasionally funny (at least to me). Always honest.

And here's how to read it:

- If you're **just a regular human with a phone and a laptop**, start with the Individual sections. Take action there. Then, if you're curious or want to understand how this all scales, read ahead and see what nightmares the "big kids" are dealing with.

- If you're a **Side-Hustler**, read both the Individual and Side-Hustler sections. This is where your empire begins, and your

attack surface explodes.

- If you're a **Mid-Cap leader**, you've graduated to the land of policy debt, vendor sprawl, and ***Shadow*** IT ("citizen developers" often rate high here). Read the first two personas too—they're how your problems start.

- If you're an **Enterprise Executive**... read the whole book, cover to cover. You own you, and you own the business. Then send it to your ***CISO*** and ask which chapters keep them up at night.

Look, I didn't come at this from an ivory tower. I've been in the trenches for over two decades. From 22+ years in the U.S. Air Force across Active-Duty, Reserve, and Air National Guard (training humans, running Information Systems, conducting Information Operations and Cyberwarfare) to leading cybersecurity programs for companies ranging from $80 million to $2.7 billion in revenue across 52 countries, I've seen the full spectrum of mistakes and miracles.

Oh, and I'm certainly not some pinnacle of cyber-knowledge... I study and learn every day. From books, peers, and articles. It's part of the trade.

So as a result: **none of this stuff surprises me anymore**.

The names change. The logos change. The executive titles change.

But the breaches? They all rhyme.

And if you want to avoid losing all your photos, avoid becoming the next headline, or the next cautionary tale in someone else's book, this one's for you.

Because security isn't someone else's job anymore. It's yours.

Let's do this.

— *Vince*

Introduction

Why You (Yes, You) Probably Suck at Cybersecurity

Let's start with a brutal truth: **You probably suck at cybersecurity.**

Don't worry—you're not alone. Most people do. (*And many of them are in charge of things they really shouldn't be.*)

From regular folks tapping through TikToks on sketchy public ***Wi-Fi*** to executives using "p@$$w@rD" plus their birthday as a password *again*, the world is filled with well-meaning humans making terrible decisions with technology. It's not always because we're dumb. It's often because no one ever taught us how to not suck at this.

Well, buckle up. That's what this book is for.

Welcome to the Cyber Sh*tshow

Perhaps that paragraph heading is a bit crass...but it's spot on. Cybercrime isn't new—it just finally got profitable enough to be everyone's full-time job. If it were a country, cybercrime would have the third- or fourth-largest GDP on Earth (depending on the analysis model), behind only the U.S. and China and possibly Germany.

You think that's an exaggeration? Both Cybersecurity Ventures and SecureWorks estimate 2024 will total out at **$9.5 Trillion in damages world-wide**. The World Economic Forum Global Cybersecurity Outlook

2025 has quantified the 2024 losses **JUST due to cyber-based financial scams to be over $1 Trillion**...that's just one sector of cybercrime. Regardless, just ask the millions of victims of ransomware, bank fraud, and identity theft who helped fund that economy... they're not arguing the total.

The idea of "computer crime" used to be a little more... quaint. Like the '80s hacker equivalent of keying someone's car.

Let's take a stroll down memory lane.

The Morris Worm (1988)

The first "big one." Robert Tappan Morris, a grad student, released what became known as the Morris Worm—a little experiment in self-replicating code that accidentally broke the early internet (or what passed for it in 1988). It spread fast, it crashed machines, and it earned Morris the dubious honor of being the first person convicted under the Computer Fraud and Abuse Act.

No profit motive. Just a guy playing around with code and accidentally proving that cybersecurity needed to be a *thing*... (and for the most part nobody did anything to prevent another one).

The AIDS Trojan (1989)

Before ransomware got sophisticated, it was hilariously bad. Dr. Joseph Popp mailed out **floppy disks** labeled "AIDS Information Introductory Diskette" to thousands of people in government and industry research and health organizations. (Yes, mailed. Like, with stamps.)

Once inserted, the disk would install a ***Trojan*** that hid file directories and demanded $189 to unlock them. The payment? Send a money order to a P.O. box in Panama.

Spoiler: almost no one paid. Popp sucked at monetizing crime, but he invented the concept of ransomware before it was cool. (Also before ***crypto***. Or PayPal. Or literally anything that would have made this remotely effective.) Others would follow, with far more devastating impact.

Silk Road (2011–2013)

Then came the Silk Road: the Amazon of drugs, fake passports, and assassins-for-hire. Built behind ***Tor*** for anonymity and ***Bitcoin*** for payments, it became the Wild West of cyber black markets.

Its creator, Ross Ulbricht (a.k.a. "Dread Pirate Roberts"), ran it like a tech startup, complete with customer support. It made millions until the feds shut it down and gave him a double life sentence (though Trump tossed him a lifeline with a partial commutation).

What mattered more than the bust was what Silk Road proved: with enough encryption, anonymity, and a dark enough corner of the internet, crime could scale. And it has.

Cybercrime: Scalable, Profitable, and Global

From there, the hits just kept coming:

- **Target** (2013): Hackers got in through an ***HVAC*** contractor and ***exfiltrated*** 40 million credit cards. The literal cost of bad vendor access.
- **WannaCry** (2017): North Korean ransomware that crippled hospitals and businesses globally, using ***NSA*** tools that were leaked online. (Yay, nation-state blowback!)
- **Colonial Pipeline** (2021): One password. One exposed ***VPN***. And 45% of the East Coast's fuel supply got shut down.

And it's not stopping. Why would it?

Cybercrime works. It's scalable. It's low-risk, high-reward. And thanks to automation, cloud infrastructure, and criminal-as-a-service marketplaces, even people with limited tech skills can get in on the action.

There are call centers in Eastern Europe *pretending to be your bank*, and they are shockingly convincing.

They Don't Care About You—But They'll Happily Destroy You

Here's what most people don't realize: cybercriminals don't need to *target* you. You're just **a soft target** that pops up in their scans.

- Your smartphone has more processing power than NASA used to put people on the moon, and you're using it to play Wordle on unsecured Wi-Fi.

- Your smart TV wants to know your location. So does your flashlight app. So does your toaster. Why? Who knows, but it's a data risk.

- That email from "Amazon Support" isn't from Amazon. But you clicked it anyway. *And gave them your login.*

The attackers don't care if you're an 83-year-old grandma in assisted living or the CEO of a billion-dollar unicorn. If they can trick you, they will. If they can profit off you, they won't hesitate. Ruining your life is an unconcerning side effect; if they can cash a check doing it, they absolutely will.

Each chapter of this book will tackle a piece of the CIS Top 18 controls and show how it applies to each of you. The problems scale, but the principles don't change. Side note: I'm not strictly following the order of the CIS Top 18 (and I cover some multiple times), so if you're familiar with it, don't lose your mind over the deviations.

This Book Is Your Guide on How to Not Suck

I'm not going to promise you nuclear-surety-grade security. I'm not going to drown you in jargon or sell you magic beans. No flashy sales rep or overconfident engineer can "prove" cybersecurity for any of us.

But by the time you're done with this book:

- You'll know how cybercriminals think (spoiler: they think you're easy).
- You'll recognize how your daily habits open the door for attacks.
- You'll learn how to fix that. Without needing a degree. Or duct tape.

You don't have to be paranoid (well, maybe a little). You just have to stop making it so stinking easy for the bad-guys.

And remember, if it's not explained well enough here, Google it. Become your own security advocate. No one else will.

Let's get started. Control #1: Know what you've got—because I promise, someone else already does.

Chapter One

Know What You've Got

CIS Control 1—Inventory and Control of Enterprise Assets

Alternate title:

"You Can't Defend What You Don't Know Exists, Genius."

Opening Story: "The Box That Shouldn't Have Been There"

They gave us the target when we arrived on station...

A mid-sized chemical processing plant in a nation we weren't on good terms with, to say the least. It wasn't the largest facility, or the most important, but it was strategic, producing an industrial compound that, if disrupted, would cause a cascading supply issue across multiple sectors, particularly their military-industrial complex.

The mission wasn't espionage. It wasn't surveillance. It was clear-cut: Cause permanent, irreversible damage. Shut the plant down.

We started, like we always did, on the outside.

The facility had a ***HMI (Human-Machine Interface)*** exposed to the public internet. A quick ***Shodan*** search and a few hours of recon gave us exactly what we needed: a login page, no ***MFA (Multi-Factor Authentication)***, no VPN. Just sitting there. Waiting.

That was mistake number one.

We cross-referenced the admin email address (received from our MI [Military Intelligence] counterparts) associated with the HMI login against known ***breach corpuses:*** old password dumps from other unrelated websites. Found five matches. Then we started ***credential stuffing***.

Tried all five as-is. No luck.

Tried a few dozen variants with the current year appended.

Bingo. We were in. So. Stupid. Simple.

Inside the HMI environment, we started mapping the network terrain. Most systems were locked down, or so it seemed. But then we found it: a box tucked away on the edge of the internal network. No alerts. No logs. No traffic. It was just...there.

Running ***Windows Server 2000. Unpatched. Unsupported. Fully privileged***. And forgotten.

That was mistake number two.

We dropped ***shell code*** on it using a decade-old ***Metasploit module***. No resistance. No endpoint detection. Nothing. It was a ***skeleton key*** into the rest of the environment.

From that foothold, the rest unraveled quickly.

We found and interrogated the ***actuators*** and ***SCADA (Supervisory Control And Data Access)*** systems, found their make, model, and ***firmware*** version. A quick Google search gave us the manuals. Public ***PDF***s. Everything we needed to understand exactly how they worked.

Then we identified the ***ICS (Integrated Control System)*** devices managing the catalyst injection at the mixing station. One of our team figured out how to issue commands that bypassed SCADA verification checks. We had direct access to the actuator control logic.

We increased the catalyst chemical in the mix by just enough to trigger a thermo-dynamic reaction. The tank went critical. Pressure blew the seams. That section of the plant? Gone.

Mission accomplished. It would take years to recover.

All because:

- An exposed login page wasn't locked down
- An admin reused a password from a decade-old breach
- A forgotten server was still online, vulnerable, and connected
- And no one had any idea it was there

Let that sink in.

This wasn't a sophisticated ***zero-day*** attack.

This wasn't elite-level cyber-warfare magic.

It was a login form, a stupid password, a forgotten server, and a Google search.

And if that can take out a chemical plant, imagine what it can do to your business.

BLUF (Bottom Line Up Front)

Every single cybersecurity incident you've ever read about, from ***ransomware*** to ***data leaks*** to that one celebrity's fridge tweeting their location, started with a simple truth:

Someone had something connected to the internet, and no one knew it was there, or if they did, they didn't monitor it for anomalous behavior.

That's it. That's the tweet.

If you don't know what devices, systems, ***endpoints***, and rogue toasters are part of your digital life or business, you are not in control.

You're just waiting for someone else to notice before you do.

Let's break it down by persona.

The Individual

"I just have a phone and a laptop!" Sure, Jan. You and me both...

Go ahead, ask the average person how many internet-connected devices they have in their house. Most will say three or four. Maybe five if they count their Xbox.

Reality? It's closer to 20–30.

That's your smart TV. Your smart speakers. Your smart thermostat. Your smart fridge, vacuum, toaster, doorbell cam, LED strip lights, sprinklers, and whatever else has snuck onto your Wi-Fi while pretending to be "smart" and make your life better.

That pile of smart junk is your attack surface.

But here's the thing: most people have no idea how to find these devices, let alone secure them.

So let's fix that.

How to Find Out What's Connected to Your Wi-Fi

Even if you've never logged into a ***router*** in your life, this is easier than you think.

Option 1: Use your router's mobile app

Most modern routers (especially from ***ISPs*** like Xfinity, AT&T, Spectrum, etc.) have mobile apps. Some common ones:

- Xfinity: In the Xfinity App go to WiFi tab, then select "Devices"
- Google Nest WiFi: In the Google Home App go to WiFi, then select "Devices"
- TP-Link: Tether app (similar path)
- Netgear: Nighthawk app (similar path)

Google your device manufacturer and see if they have an app.

What to do (rename stuff):

- Open the app and find the "connected devices" list in the router.
- Go through each one and try to identify it. Most names will be garbage like ESP-DF8BA0 or android-31d831. That's normal.
- Rename each one so you know what it is ("Emma's iPad", "Living Room Roku", etc.).
- If you don't recognize it, rename it to "UNKNOWN_EVIL" and investigate later.

Option 2: Log into your router directly

- On a browser (while connected to your WiFi), go to: http://192.168.1.1 or http://192.168.0.1 (common defaults)
- Login (your router sticker probably has the username/password: usually admin/admin or admin/password, which is... horrifying). Change that default username/password to something reasonable. Length matters more than complexity (go for 15-20 characters), and avoid using just dictionary words.

- Look for a "Connected Devices" or "Device List" section
- Then follow the renaming process above.

How to Update Your Home Router (and Why You Must)

Outdated routers are one of the most common ways bad guys walk right into your network. Here's how to fix that:

- Log into your router (see Option 2 above).
- Find the Firmware Update or Software Update section.
- It might be under "Administration," "System," or "Advanced."
- Click "Check for Updates" or "Update Now."
- Then Enable "***auto-updates***".

If your router doesn't have auto-updates, replace it with one that does. Seriously.

Pro Tip: If your router was provided by your ISP and it doesn't let you update firmware, or it hasn't updated in over a year—ask for a new one, or go buy your own (Ubiquiti, Asus, and eero are all solid choices).

Set Up a Guest Network (This One is Big)

Your Wi-Fi is sacred. Stop letting your guests, smart junk, and random devices rub elbows with your laptop.

Why set up a guest network?

- ***Segments*** risky devices from your real stuff
- Limits what your guests/devices can see or access
- Keeps malware from jumping around like it's a house party

How to set it up:

- Log into your router (you're a pro now).
- Look for a setting called Guest Network or Guest Wi-Fi.
- Turn it on.
- Give it a fun but obvious name like "VirusHoldingPen" or "UntrustedStuff".
- Enable ***client isolation*** if available (prevents devices from talking to each other).
- Set a strong password (as described above, and keep it significantly different from your main Wi-Fi, don't just add "123" to the end of that other password... I know you were thinking that).

What goes on your guest network:

- Smart TVs
- ***IoT*** devices (light bulbs, cameras, thermostats)
- Kids' tablets
- Visitors' phones and laptops

What stays on your main network:

- Your personal laptop or desktop
- Phones you use for banking/work
- ***Network-attached storage (NAS)***, printers with sensitive docs (we'll talk about updating printers later)

Digital Decluttering: What to Unplug, Update, or Replace

If you find something on your network and you can't figure out what it is:

- Kick if off your network (*if it breaks something, at least you know what it was)
- Update it if it has a companion app or firmware setting
- Replace it if it's ancient and hasn't had an update since Obama was in office

And seriously: **change default passwords**.
Your router, your cameras, your doorbell.
If it's still set to "admin" / "admin", congratulations, you just invited the internet to your housewarming party.

Optional (But Awesome): Create *Virtual Local Area Networks (VLANs)*... If You're a Little Nerdy

If you're even a little adventurous, some routers (like Ubiquiti's UniFi or Asuswrt-Merlin) let you set up VLANs, basically creating totally separate zones for your smart gear vs. your personal devices.

This is next-level segmentation.
Not required, but if you're feeling spicy, it'll add serious muscle to your home network security.

One Last Thing: Let's Talk Passwords (aka The Keys to Your Entire Digital Life)

You can lock down your home Wi-Fi like Fort Knox, but if you're still using Fluffy123! for every account (and you likely have dozens if not hundreds), you're basically handing your attackers the keys and a bag of snacks for the road trip.

Here's what you need to know, and do, without needing to be a tech wizard:

Use a Password Manager

Seriously. This is one of the easiest, highest-impact things you can do.

A good ***password manager***:

- Stores all your passwords in one secure vault
- Suggests strong, unique passwords for each site or device
- Syncs across your devices
- Saves your butt when a site gets breached (because only that password needs to change, as all of your 150+ passwords are unique)

Recommended options:

- Bitwarden (Free, open-source, super solid)
- 1Password (Sleek and family-friendly)
- Dashlane (Great UX, decent autofill)

If you're the "I don't trust putting my passwords online" type...I get it. But odds are your current setup is way worse... likely online, or on your phone or computer.

At Least Use a Password Book (Yes, Like with a Pen)

Let's be blunt:

A written password book, kept in a drawer at home, is way safer than an unprotected Excel file called Passwords2022.xlsx on your desktop, or worse, your Google Drive.

No one's robbing your house to get your Netflix password.

But malware can absolutely snatch that unencrypted spreadsheet the moment your computer gets compromised.

If you're not ready to commit to a password manager:

- Buy a small notebook (yes, analog style)
- Write down your accounts and passwords neatly (ensuring they are truly unique across accounts)
- Store it somewhere that's not taped to your monitor, and not obviously visible to others
- Update it when you change things (and yes, you should be changing things)

And AGAIN: Stop Reusing Passwords

If you've used the same password (or even the same base password with various modifications) across more than one sit...stop it.

A breach in one site means attackers will try that same combo on every other site you own.

It's called credential stuffing, and it works terrifyingly well... Remember the story at the start of this chapter, only adding the current year to the known passwords and... boom!

Use a unique password for every major account (email, banking, social media).

Even just your top five accounts is a massive improvement.

The Bare Minimum Setup for Not Sucking:

- Use a password manager, or a physical password book
- Use strong, unique passwords (even if you don't remember them,

let your manager do the work)

- Never store passwords in your browser, Notes app, online storage, or email
- Enable MFA where possible, especially on email, banking, and cloud storage

Quick Win for Individuals:

Task	Why It Matters	Tool/How-To
Lock down router & Wi-Fi	Prevent outside attacks on home network	Router admin panel + firmware updates
Secure passwords	Avoid credential stuffing and ***brute-forcing***	Password manager (Bitwarden, 1Password)
Scan your networks	Know what's connected	Router App or Admin Panel (Google it if needed)
Separate trusted/untrusted devices	Rename/remove unknowns, Isolate sketchy IoT junk	Device name features, Guest networks, VLANs
Practice ***digital hygiene***	Lower exposure to scams and theft	Cloud backup + basic self-audits

The Side-Hustler

"It's just a little Etsy shop, not Fort Knox."

Attackers don't care. If you accept payments, have a site, store user info, or simply care if your stuff stays accessible, you're a target.

And all the stuff above in the "Individual" section applies to you too. Those are all entry points into **you**. And **you** have entry points into your shop.

What You Should Do:

- List all your tools, platforms, and devices… all of them
- Use a password manager just for business (keep your personal one separate)
- Scan your site with Sucuri, ***OWASP ZAP*** or Mozilla Observatory (Google the results, fix what matters)
- Keep your ***POS (Point-of-Sale)***/payment systems up to date
- Segment your business laptop from home devices

Quick Wins for Side-Hustlers

Task	**Why It Matters**	**How-To**
Inventory your ***stack***	Know your exposure	Write down every platform/device
Use strong credentials	Protect accounts	Password manager + MFA
Scan your site	Spot obvious issues	Sucuri, Mozilla Observatory, ZAP
Segment your network	Prevent device crossover risk	Guest network or VLAN
Stop local data storage	Prevent theft/loss	Use secure cloud storage

The Mid-Cap Boss

"We've got a decent IT guy. He handles that stuff."

You've outgrown the "one IT hero" model. Asset sprawl, vendor access, and invisible systems will wreck you. It's time to put on the big-boy/big-girl pants and build a defensible stack.

And of course, you can't defend what you don't see. Add the following guidance to all you learned above, and start rubbing shoulders with the cybersecurity side of business... or you can wait till the ransom note appears on everyone's screen (one-star, not recommended).

What You Should Do:

- Build a real ***asset inventory*** with an asset tracking tool (Snipe-IT, Rumble, Asset Tiger). You'll need a complete list of all of your computers, routers, printers, etc... basically anything with a serial number.

- Implement ***ticketing*** systems (Freshdesk, Zoho, Spiceworks) to track work requests, security ***patch*** efforts, etc.

- Patch regularly with real cadence and emergency handling (prioritize based on risk to the company)

- Know your regulatory environment (***GDPR, PCI, HIPAA***, etc.)
- Train your team using ***phishing*** simulations (more covered later on)
- Define internal ***fraud controls*** and ***financial verification*** processes

Quick Wins for Mid-Cap Bosses

Task	**Why It Matters**	**How-To**
Track assets automatically	Unknown Shadow IT kills visibility	Rumble, Asset Tiger
Formalize patching	Close known doors	WSUS, PDQ Deploy
Phishing training	Reduce human error risk	Gophish, KnowBe4
Add ticketing system	Audit trails + IT workload view	Freshdesk, Zoho, Spiceworks
Define financial controls	Prevent fraud and scams	Dual auth, known contact policies

The Enterprise Executive

"We've got teams for that."

Leadership is not immunity. It's exposure.

Your teams will only be secure to the extent you show commitment to security. If you're the one constantly bringing in an Alexa, a personal iPad, a smart speaker, a smart humidifier (etc., ad nauseum), then, your teams won't respect the policy telling them they can't stand up a rogue server somewhere for some "pet project"... (refer back to our opening story).

If you've not implemented all the stuff in the "Individual" section above, do it. It's embarrassing when your cyber team comes across your publicly exposed, outdated printer because it's part of a ***botnet.***

You set the tone. They'll play the music.

What You Should Do:

- Acknowledge that asset inventory isn't "just IT's job."
- Demand real ***dashboards,*** not slide decks with platitudes. Real time security metrics with change-over-time tracking tell the story you want.
- Tie cyber to business strategy (esp. ***M&A, BC/DR, third-party risk***)

- Set the ***IAM (Identity and Access Management)*** tone: use Multi-Factor Authentication (MFA), follow policies, and complete your own training

- Ask uncomfortable questions about ***visibility*** and ***risk*** (i.e., Can we tell what IPs are attempting to connect to our servers? Are our internet exposed servers protected behind a ***WAF (Web Application Firewall)***? How can we tell if our data is modified erroneously?)

Quick Wins for Enterprise Executives

Task	Why It Matters	Action
Mandate real-time visibility	Avoid flying blind	Require live dashboards for security metrics
Make cyber board-level	Make it strategic	Add to board/risk committee
Lead by example	Shape security culture	Use MFA, take training, ask questions
Fund the people AND tools	Avoid "***shelfware***" risk	Prioritize ***FTE (Full Time Employee)*** resourcing
Review your personal exposure	You're a target too	Audit devices/accounts/home network

Real-World Fails

- A senior exec used personal Dropbox to share Human Resource (HR) files...accidentally leaked ***PII (Personally Identifiable Information)***.
- A legacy system with default creds was breached...unknown asset from an M&A.
- A junior staffer installed Dropbox and synced sensitive data to a personal account.
- A CFO's home printer was publicly exposed via ***UPnP...*** connected to her company laptop.

Final Thought for Chapter 1

A huge number of breaches start with a single, usually stupid asset that someone forgot.

Not every asset is dangerous, but every unknown asset is.

You can't protect what you can't see.

You can't patch what you don't track.

And you can't sleep well if your environment is an uncontrolled mess of devices, systems, and connections.

Know what you've got.

Or someone else will find it for you...and not in a good way.

Quick Wins by Persona

Persona	Quick Win	Why It Matters	Tool/How-To
Individual	Log in to your Router	Knowing this system is the foundation to your personal IT world. All that smart crap you own connects to this.	Google your router manufacturer and look up your device. Follow the instructions.
Side-Hustler	Start playing with OWASP ZAP	Knowing what your site *really* looks like to an attacker	www.owasp.org search for ZAP
Mid-Cap Boss	Build your asset inventory	Once you know what you actually have, you can start to deal with it.	Rumble, Asset Tiger
Enterprise Exec	Integrate Cyber into your business processes	Cyber fails can cripple, or worse, kill your business. Ignoring it won't help	Make it a line-item for each Exec Council and/or Board meeting. Educate yourself on what matters.

Chapter Two

Know What It's Running

CIS Control 2—Inventory and Control of Software Assets

Alternate Title:

"Software = Soft Target"

Opening Story: Just One Login

It started with something so simple, so normal, it barely registered as a risk.

An employee at one of the most security-forward companies in the world, Okta, sat down at their workstation and signed into their personal Google account.

Not a big deal, right? People do it all the time. Check some personal email, maybe view a shared doc, log out. Harmless.

Except this time, it wasn't.

That single login into an un-managed ***SaaS (Software-as-a-Service)*** created an opening, a chink in the armor, that would eventually compromise **134 companies**, including some of the most well-known names in cybersecurity: **1Password. Cloudflare. BeyondTrust.**

This was 2023. The attacker didn't use a zero-day. There was no novel exploit or sophisticated malware chain. Just old-school ***session hijacking***, enabled by an unmanaged, unsanctioned, unmonitored use of software on a company device.

Here's what happened:

The personal Google account created a ***trusted context*** on the machine. When the attacker gained access (possibly via malware, possibly by ***token theft***)they found themselves inside Okta's **customer support system**.

And that's where the real damage began.

Stored within the support environment were ***browser session tokens*** for a number of Okta customers. With those tokens in hand, the attacker didn't need usernames, passwords, or even MFA.

They simply reused the stolen session tokens to impersonate legitimate users.

Click. Full access.

By the time Okta publicly acknowledged the breach, the attacker had been in the system for **20 days**.

During that time, they quietly moved laterally, targeting Okta's customers: companies who had trusted Okta to manage the front door of their identities. Some of those companies were security vendors themselves. And they got hit hard.

It wasn't a vulnerability (or vuln for short) in code.

It wasn't a firewall misconfiguration.

It wasn't a nation-state with advanced persistence tools.

It was one employee, signing into **one personal Google account**, on a corporate device, using a browser with no oversight and no policy enforcement.

This wasn't a technology failure. It was a **visibility failure**.

The software was legitimate, but unmanaged.
The session was valid.
The system was blind.

And that's exactly how attackers win.

Lesson: You can't secure what you don't know is running.
And software (apps, browsers, ***plugins***, ***scripts***, ***containers***) is just as much an attack surface as servers.

BLUF (Bottom Line Up Front)

If you don't track your software, someone else will.
And that "someone else" isn't likely to send you a helpful inventory spreadsheet.

CIS Control 2 exists because untracked software = unmanaged vulnerabilities.From sketchy ***browser extensions*** to rogue developer tools, every unmonitored install or connection to unmanaged SaaS is a potential breach waiting to happen.

You can't just worry about servers anymore.
You have to worry about what's *on* the servers...and laptops, and phones, and SaaS platforms, and ***GitHub*** repos.

Let's break it down by persona.

The Individual

"It's just a browser extension, how bad could it be?"

Oh, you sweet summer child. Let's see what you've got:

- A free PDF converter that somehow has 94 million installs in 2 months and a 4.9 rating
- A sketchy "Coupon Hunter" Chrome extension that wants access to all your tabs and browsing history
- "Flashlight++" on your Android phone that asks for microphone and contact access (??)

They all count.
And if you're not managing them, you're opening doors you don't even know about.

Here's the thing: **free apps aren't free.**
You're paying with your data, your device performance, or your attack surface.

And you don't even know what's running half the time:

- Background services from old apps you forgot to uninstall
- Auto-start junk from your printer software

- Extensions syncing across devices without your knowledge

The bloat associated with modern software is epic, and it takes a savant with a thousand spreadsheets to keep up.

What To Do (For Real Humans):

- **Audit your browser extensions:** Go to chrome://extensions and/or your other browser's add-ons page. Delete anything you don't *explicitly* recognize or use.

- **Check your installed apps list:** On phones *and* laptops. If you haven't used it in 90 days, delete it... (it's like cleaning out your garage).

- **Use a trusted antivirus/*EDR (Endpoint Detection and Response)* product** that alerts you to risky behaviors, not just malware. And yes, you'll need to pay for it (remember my comment on "free" above?).

- **Turn off auto-install syncing** across browsers (especially Chrome).

- **Don't install software you don't understand**. Especially from Reddit threads.

Quick Win for Individuals:

Task	Why It Matters	Tool/How-To
Review installed software monthly	Kill off abandoned apps (aka vulnerabilities)	Device settings + browser extension managers ("Extension Manager" or "Extensity")
Remove unused apps	Shrink your attack surface	Uninstall via App Store/Settings
Update everything	Patch vulnerabilities automatically	Auto-update settings

The Side-Hustler

"I just use a few plugins for my store..."

And that's enough to give a ***PHP shell*** to a guy in North Korea.

One vulnerable ***WordPress plugin*** can wreck your whole operation.

When you're running a Shopify store, a WordPress blog, or a Squarespace landing page, everything is an "add-on."

But every plugin, widget, extension, and no-code automation increases your risk.

Most side-hustlers install stuff with no vetting, no updates, and no plan to remove it later.

That abandoned WordPress plugin from 2018? It's vulnerable. That WooCommerce extension from some random developer? It has more permissions than it needs. If it hasn't been updated in a year, kill it and find a new one to do that job.

Attackers don't care how big your store is.
They care if they can skim credit cards, plant malware, hold it for ransom, or boost ***SEO (Search Engine Optimization)*** for their shady websites.

What To Do (Yes, Even If You're "Just Selling Stickers"):

- Track every plugin, extension, app, and integration connected to your site.

- Update religiously:
  - ***CMS (Content Management System)*** platforms like WordPress, Shopify, Squarespace push updates for a reason.
  - Update plugins and themes, not just core.
  - Uninstall what you don't use (or what hasn't been updated since Obama was President)
- Vet new installs carefully:
  - <u>Popular ≠ Safe</u>
  - Check update history. Check the dev team. Check recent reviews.
  - Google the name of the plugin + "vulnerability" before you install anything. **Virus Total** (www.virustotal.com) is a great resource for checking out software.
- Use security plugins:
  - Sucuri, Wordfence (for WordPress), and basic web firewalls can help catch shady installs.
- Install a basic WAF (like Cloudflare's free plan)
- Disable directory listing and file editing in your CMS
- Regularly scan your site:
  - Mozilla Observatory

  - OWASP ZAP
  - Sucuri SiteCheck

If you're using browser-based tools like Zapier, IFTTT, or social automation, make sure you're using:

- Unique ***API keys*** per integration
- MFA on your accounts
- Documentation for what's plugged into what

Shadow software in your side hustle will still ruin your day—and possibly your customer base.

Quick Win for Side-Hustlers:

Task	Why It Matters	Tool/How-To
Inventory your plugins/extensions	Know what's running	Spreadsheet + monthly review
Update CMS core and plugins	Prevent known ***exploits***	Auto-updates where possible
Run site security scans	Catch hidden vulnerabilities	Sucuri, Mozilla Observatory

The Mid-Cap Boss

"We standardize our software. It's all approved by IT."

Are you sure?

Because here's what's really happening:

- Sales downloaded a new call recording app "for convenience"
- Marketing signed up for a webinar tool that stores attendee data in Europe (and didn't tell Legal)
- A junior developer spun up a public code repo on GitHub that now has your internal documentation in plaintext
- Someone in HR connected a third-party payroll tool with full access to your employee directory, or even better, it includes an AI Chatbot that can't discriminate role permissions.

And guess what? Your **EDR agent doesn't detect any of it**.

Shadow SaaS and unapproved tools are exploding, and unless you're monitoring browser-based usage, cloud integrations, and app-to-app ***OAuth*** authorizations, **you are not in control.**

What To Do (Without Going Full Totalitarian):

- Use SaaS discovery tools to build a software inventory (Microsoft

Defender for Cloud Apps [free for some 365 plans], Torli, DoControl, Netskope):

  - SaaS, installed apps, cloud services.
  - Everything. Continuously.

- Conduct browser plugin audits via G Suite Admin
- Use an MDM (Mobile Device Management) platform:
  - Intune, Jamf, Kandji, etc.
- Standardize deployments:
  - ***Gold images*** for endpoints.
  - ***Hardened container templates*** for cloud.
- Implement an approval process:
  - New software requests go through security review.
  - Require justification and expiration dates on all app approvals
- Scan codebases and containers:
  - Trivy, Snyk, OWASP Dependency-Check.
- Regularly review connected OAuth apps (Google Admin > Security > API Controls)
- Train teams to self-police:
  - Developers especially.

Quick Win for Mid-Cap Bosses:

Task	Why It Matters	Tool/How-To
Inventory SaaS and on-prem apps	Identify risky sprawl	***CMDB (Configuration Management Data Base)***, SaaS Management Platforms
Lock down software installs	Reduce unauthorized software	***MDM (Mobile Device Management)*** enforcement policies
Scan containers and codebases	Prevent supply chain attacks	Trivy, Snyk, GitHub security scans

The Enterprise Executive

"We're ISO27001 certified. We have it all documented."

Cool story, bro.

Now ask yourself:

- How current is that software inventory?
- How often are supply chain attacks simulated?
- How are low-code integrations tracked?
- How many "temporary" SaaS apps are still active, and still have access?

Yeah, you're likely not getting good answers...

The 2023 Okta breach (yeah, the one we just talked about) wasn't caused by malware. It was caused by **untracked software behavior** and a personal login session on a corporate device.

You cannot manage software inventory with a checkbox.

You need **dynamic, real-time visibility** across all layers:

- Endpoints
- Cloud workloads

- Web traffic
- OAuth integrations

And here's the kicker: it's not just about **knowing** what's there. It's about **controlling** what's allowed to be there.

Enterprise-Grade Actions (No More Excuses):

- Enforce ***SAM (Software Asset Management)***:
  - With active, quarterly audits, using real tools, not just Excel sheets.
- Tie software inventory into risk registers:
  - Map software to criticality. Prioritize patching and replacement.
  - Prioritize patching, replacement, mitigation based on business function, data exposure, and likelihood (yeah, that old Impact / Likelihood graph)
- Monitor third-party risk:
  - Use services like SecurityScorecard, UpGuard, Bitsight.
  - Conduct quarterly app reviews with business units—remove anything you don't need.
- Secure your dev pipeline:
  - ***SAST (Static application security testing) and DAST (Dynamic Application Security Testing)***.

  - Dependency scanning (***SBOM***s mandatory).
  - Threat model 3rd-party integrations.
- Review exceptions quarterly:
  - Every "just this once" install gets reviewed. Risk gets signed off by a VP
  - Kill abandoned apps ruthlessly.

SaaS Security Posture Management (SSPM) solutions such as AppOmni, Adaptive Shield, Grip, or Obsidian allow you to audit and enforce SaaS configuration. It works on the big players (e.g., SalesForce, Snowflake, ServiceNow); but most generally have gaps on the smaller more niche SaaS providers.

Regardless, these types of tools do give some enforcement and visibility into SaaS - Which most security folks agree is significantly underestimated with respect to enterprise risk. Remember, just because it's SaaS doesn't mean it's not yours when it comes to impact when things go south.

Quick Win for Enterprise Execs:

Task	Why It Matters	Tool/How-To
Mandate live software inventories	Real-time risk visibility	Asset discovery tools, CMDB integrations
Secure dev pipelines + dependencies	Stop supply chain compromises	Dependency-checks, SBOMs, threat modeling
Monitor vendor software risks	Mitigate third-party vulnerabilities	Security ratings services, contract clauses

Real-World Fails

- A Chrome extension used by the sales team was purchased by an adware company and turned into spyware overnight. No alerts. No updates. Just a quiet exfiltration of ***CRM*** data.
- A marketing intern installed an unlicensed copy of Adobe CC using a cracked installer. That "installer" came bundled with a keylogger...total pwnage.
- A dev team was using a GitHub-hosted dependency that got hijacked after the maintainer sold the domain. The attacker injected malicious code into a production build.

Final Thought for Chapter 2

Your attackers know exactly what software versions you're running. (Trust me, they're scanning and enumerating you right now.)

If you don't know what you've installed, or what your team has installed for you, you are officially flying blind.

Hope isn't a strategy. Inventory is.

Track it. Patch it. Kill it if you don't need it.

Quick Wins by Persona for Chapter 2

Persona	Quick Win	Tool/Tip
Individual	Audit browser extensions	chrome://extensions, Firefox Add-ons
Side-Hustler	Remove unused WordPress plugins/themes	Dashboard > Plugins > Deactivate/Delete
Mid-Cap Boss	Review OAuth connections across departments	Google Admin > API Controls
Enterprise Exec	Implement browser extension policies via MDM	***Intune, JAMF, GPO***

Chapter Three

Lock It Down, or Watch It Leak

CIS Control 3—Data Protection

Alternate Title:
"Oops, I Shared the Payroll Spreadsheet with the Whole Company"

Opening Story: "Make It Just Go Away... Click 'Approve'"

In 2022, a teenager breached Uber.

No elite hacking skills. No nation-state tools. Just persistence, open-source research, and one exhausted employee who ultimately clicked "Approve" on his phone's authenticator app to make an annoying stream of prompts go away.

It started with a stolen password, leaked from a third-party breach and reused across accounts. The attacker hit the login screen, triggered an MFA request, and then sent another...

And another.

And another.

And another.

Eventually, the Uber employee tapped "Approve."

Maybe it was late. Maybe he thought it was a glitch. Maybe he just wanted the pop-ups to stop.

Either way, the attacker was in.

From there, it wasn't hard. Uber's internal systems were over-permissioned and under-protected. It was an information free-for-all. The attacker found PowerShell scripts with admin credentials embedded in plaintext. Accessed internal dashboards. Reached Slack, ***AWS (Amazon Web Services)***, G Suite, and even Uber's vulnerability reports. A literal buffet of data.

All because:

- MFA fatigue wasn't accounted for
- Credentials weren't stored securely
- **Sensitive data** was just sitting around, accessible to people who didn't need it

Uber got lucky. The attacker wasn't destructive, just noisy. But the reputational damage, internal disruption, and very public embarrassment? Permanent.

Lesson:

You can't protect what you don't label.

You can't secure what you let everyone touch.

And you definitely can't defend what's been rotting in your shared drive since 2018.

BLUF (Bottom Line Up Front)

Data is like water.

It leaks. It seeps. It finds every crack you didn't know existed, and once it's out, you're not getting it back. Ever.

Every device, every app, every employee, and every integration is a potential leaky pipe.

If you don't know:

- What sensitive data you have
- Where it lives
- Who can access it
- And how it moves around

...then you are not protecting it.

CIS Control 3 exists because most breaches aren't caused by hackers breaking in.

They're caused by data walking out the front door, unprotected, over-shared, and exposed through systems that never should've had access in the first place.

Let's look at how this all plays out at every level.

The Individual

"It's just my personal stuff."

Let's talk about your digital junk drawer.

You've got:

- Tax documents in your email inbox
- Bank statements in your Downloads folder
- A photo of your driver's license in iCloud because you needed it once, two years ago

Oh, and don't forget:

- Your browser autofill settings store your address, credit cards, maybe even your SSN
- Your browser history is synced across devices (yes, even the work laptop you checked Amazon on)
- Your cloud storage is wide open because you never reviewed your sharing settings

Your personal digital footprint isn't just a trail, it's a crime scene waiting to happen. And while researchers haven't nailed down the exact size in bytes of the average American digital bulk, here's a preview of the mess:

- 93% of Americans are online, clocking over **6 hours a day** on average.
- The average person has **6.7 social media accounts**, each one leaking metadata like a cracked faucet.
- The average website has **32 tracking scripts**. That's not browsing, that's being watched.
- Global data creation is expected to hit **175 zettabytes** in 2025. Spoiler: you're part of the problem.

Is it out of control? Absolutely.
But you *can* control how much sensitive data you actively hang out in the wind.

What to Fix Right Now:

- Audit your cloud storage (Google Drive, iCloud, Dropbox):
    - Check shared files
    - Revoke old links
    - Remove sensitive stuff that doesn't need to live there. If it hasn't sparked joy (or relevance) since 2019, delete it. You're not running a museum.
- Turn off auto-upload from messaging apps (especially WhatsApp and Messenger)

- Clean out your Downloads folder
- Use secure notes in your password manager, not the Notes app
- Shred your metadata:
    - Strip location and ID tags (EXIF data) from files and photos you share publicly

Just because it's "your" data doesn't mean it's off-limits. "I don't have anything worth stealing" is a fairy tale. They want to either ransom your digital life, or take it over... and attackers love low-effort wins.

Quick Win for Individuals:

Task	Why It Matters	Tool/How-To
Audit cloud storage shares	Prevent oversharing of sensitive data	Google Drive/Dropbox sharing settings
Turn off auto-upload in messaging apps	Limit cloud exposure	App settings (WhatsApp, Messenger)
Strip metadata from files/photos	Avoid leaking location or device info	Exiftool, built-in OS tools

The Side-Hustler

"Nobody's targeting me—I'm too small to care about."

Wrong.

You collect:

- Names
- Emails
- Shipping addresses
- Payment data (even if it's through Stripe or PayPal)

And if you're not careful, that's all discoverable; by accident or by attacker.

A single misconfigured Google Form, Shopify export, or mailing list tool can leave your customers exposed.

And Magecart credit card stealer? It'll happily squeeze between your storefront and your PCI-compliant payment processor—because you thought "set it and forget it" was a security strategy.

What to Lock Down:

- **Email Lists**:

  - Make sure exported ***CSVs*** don't sit around in cloud drives forever
  - Never email customer lists to yourself "just in case." That *is* the case—of identity theft waiting to happen.
- **Form Builders**:
  - Use privacy-respecting platforms (Typeform, Jotform)
  - Disable public form results
  - Avoid collecting more info than you need
- **Public Sharing**:
  - Don't share Google Drive folders with "Anyone with the link"
  - Don't post invoice screenshots or sales dashboards on social media
- **Privacy Policy**:
  - Yes, even you need one...especially if you collect EU data (GDPR alert)
- **Email Hygiene**:
  - Use a dedicated business email, not your personal Gmail
  - Consider privacy-first email like ProtonMail or Zoho. Google doesn't need to read everything.
  - Turn on MFA like your digital life depends on it...because it

does.

- **Website(s):**
    - Regularly scan your website with a vulnerability scanner. OWASP ZAP, BurpSuite free edition, Immuniweb mobile app scanner, etc.

You might be a one-person business, but the internet doesn't care.

As far as attackers are concerned, you're a low-cost jackpot with zero security team.

Own your role. Protect your data. Or get used to writing apology emails.

Quick Wins for Side-Hustlers:

Task	Why It Matters	Tool/How-To
Lock down email exports and forms	Protect customer data	Google Forms/Typeform settings
Secure business email and apps	Prevent account hijacking	MFA + email domain separation
Audit public sharing	Reduce accidental leaks	Cloud storage and social media settings

The Mid-Cap Boss

"We encrypt everything... I think?"

You've got customer data, employee records, financials, contracts, IP, and regulatory exposure (aka a full-blown data risk cocktail).

And here's the kicker: half the time, you don't even know where that data lives.

- Old file shares with stale permissions
- Abandoned SharePoint sites
- Slack messages with sensitive attachments
- Email inboxes with six years of HR docs (spoiler: your inbox is not a document repository...stop treating it like one)

Oh, and let's not forget the contractors and interns who had *just enough* access to create a compliance nightmare.

You don't need a breach to be at risk. You just need **visibility gaps and too much trust**.

What to Implement Before Someone Asks for "The Report":

- Build a data inventory:
    - Start with ***data classification:*** What's sensitive, confidential,

or internal-use-only?

  - Inventory **where that data is stored**:
    - Shared drives
    - Collaboration platforms (Google Workspace, M365, Dropbox, Box), and likely in personal accounts
    - Local endpoints (laptops, NAS, etc.)
  - Identify who has access, and **why**
- Permissions Review:
  - Run a **quarterly audit** of who has access to what
  - Implement ***Just Enough Access (JEA):*** No more "Marketing has full access to Finance because it's easier that way"
  - Lock down **file-sharing defaults** (e.g., remove "Anyone with the link" options)
- Apply Basic ***DLP (Data Loss Prevention)***
  - Use **Microsoft Purview** (included in some M365 plans) to auto-label sensitive data to cover your Microsoft footprint
  - Use **Google Workspace DLP rules** to flag or block ***PII*** leaving via Gmail or Drive
  - Roll out **endpoint protection with *data-aware policies*** (CrowdStrike, SentinelOne, or even Bitdefender

GravityZone)

- Write or configure cloud controls to detect data moving out of your cloud erroneously
- Lock down outbound traffic like your data's trying to sneak out the side door...because it probably is

- Train your humans:
  - Teach employees the difference between **sharing with teammates vs. "the whole freaking internet"**
  - Build a **sensitive data checklist** for HR, Finance, and Legal
  - Remind everyone: **Email is forever. So is that spreadsheet you shared in Slack.**

Quick Wins for Mid-Cap Bosses:

Task	Why It Matters	Tool/How-To
Build a data inventory	Know where your risk lives	*M365*/***GCP*** security centers
Review access permissions	Minimize accidental exposure	IAM/DLP reviews quarterly
Apply basic DLP policies	Catch leaks before they happen	Microsoft Purview, Google Workspace

The Enterprise Executive

"We have a data governance program."

Good. But how real is it?

Governance isn't a binder full of policies. It's measurable, enforced, and driving action across departments.

Do you know if:

- Anyone actually follows your policies? How do you verify?
- That "temp contractor" from Q1 still has access to your M&A folder? Yeah. You're funding their side hustle now.
- Your SharePoint permissions are set to "open buffet mode" by default?

Here's the deal: at enterprise scale, ***data sprawl* is inevitable,** but unmanaged data sprawl is a reputational time bomb.

Attackers don't need to break your defenses, they just need to jiggle the one door you forgot to lock.

(Looking at you, Uber.)

What You Should Be Asking:

"Where's Our *Crown-Jewel Data*?"

- Has it been mapped?
- Is it classified?
- Is it encrypted at rest (***volume encrypted*** for general, and ***file/field level encrypted*** for sensitive) *and* in transit ***(TLS)***?

"What Tools Do We Actually Use to Protect Data?"

- Do we have **real-time DLP** across email, endpoints, and cloud apps?
- Are we tracking **data movement**, not just system access?
- Can we produce an **audit report** on short notice?

"Who Has Access, and Why?"

- Is access based on **roles**, or on **who yelled loudest to IT last quarter**?
- Do execs *really* need full access to raw CRM exports?
- Are service accounts and third-party integrations documented, or are they just quietly doing whatever they want in prod?

"How Do We Handle Insider Risk?"

- Are we monitoring for **exfiltration behaviors** (e.g., massive downloads, off-hours sharing)?
- Do we have a **response *playbook*** for insider threats?
- When was the last time we tested it?

If your DLP alerts go unread, your classification tags are "just vibes," and your file shares resemble a flea market, you're not governing data, you're crossing your fingers and lighting a candle.

Quick Wins for Enterprise Execs:

Task	Why It Matters	Tool/How-To
Mandate data classification enforcement	Link governance to tech	DLP, ***CASB***, cloud tagging tools
Enforce vendor data protection evidence	Mitigate third-party risk	Contract clauses, annual audits
Integrate data mapping into M&A	Prevent inherited disasters	M&A playbook updates

Real-World Fails

- An employee uploaded a CSV of 10,000 customers to their personal Google Drive "just to work from home"
- A terminated contractor still had access to a marketing ***S3 bucket*** for 14 months, containing launch materials for a still-secret product
- A misconfigured Google Group exposed internal legal documents to *all employees* (and one very surprised intern)

Final Thought for Chapter 3

You can't protect what you don't label.

You can't secure what you don't control.

And you can't fix what's leaking if you don't even know where the pipes are.

Get your data house in order...before someone else rearranges it for you.

Quick Wins by Persona for Chapter 3

Persona	Quick Win	Why It Matters	Tool/How-To
Individual	Audit cloud storage shares	Prevent oversharing of sensitive data	Google Drive/Dropbox sharing settings
Side-Hustler	Lock down forms + file exports	Avoid accidental exposure of customer data	Jotform/Typeform + secured cloud storage
Mid-Cap Boss	Build a lightweight data inventory	Enables visibility and better access control	Excel + M365/Google Workspace audits
Enterprise Exec	Enforce classification + DLP	Stops data loss before it starts	Microsoft Purview, Google DLP, endpoint DLP tools

Chapter Four

Stop Clicking "Next-Next-Finish"

CIS Control 4—Secure Configuration of Enterprise Assets and Software

Alternate Title:

"Congratulations, You Just Deployed a Dumpster Fire"

Opening Story: "The Login Was 'admin / admin'... Because Of Course It Was"

A few years back, a regional hospital in the U.S. suffered a ransomware attack that took entire departments offline. Patient records inaccessible. Lab results delayed. ER intake moved to pen and paper. Chaos.

The entry point?

A network-connected radiology device that hadn't been patched in three years (any one of the patches would have removed a default, hidden account set by the manufacturer).

The credentials to that account?

admin / admin

The problem?

The guy who ran the install and left 30 minutes later didn't disable that account, and nobody in IT ever thought to patch the device...they probably never even checked for patches.

Worse: the device was on the hospital's totally flat main network. No segmentation. No alerts. No restrictions. Just a medical-grade, vulnerable Windows box sitting there, unpatched, wide open.

The attacker found it through a basic Shodan scan, logged in, dropped ransomware, and let it do its thing.

One misconfigured system.

One skipped step.

Millions in damage.

Secure configuration isn't sexy.

But neither is explaining to the board why your ER is offline and someone named CryptoGoblin wants $5 million in Bitcoin.

Lesson:

Secure configuration isn't sexy, but neither is explaining to the board why your entire operation is being held for ransom.

BLUF (Bottom Line Up Front)

Secure configuration isn't hard, but it is annoying, and that's why most people skip it.

They hit "Next" until the install completes. They leave the defaults (because clearly, "admin/admin" was tested by security engineers everywhere... right?). They never change the password. They never turn off ***test ports.*** And then they walk away like it's someone else's problem.

CIS Control 4 exists because most environments aren't hacked...they're just left wide open by lazy, default, insecure settings.

Whether it's:

- A cloud storage bucket with public read permissions
- A firewall rule that allows "Any/Any"
- A server with ***RDP (Remote Desktop Protocol)*** wide open
- Or an IoT device phoning home to some sketchy country code trying to order malware off a menu

...the attacker doesn't need to "break in." They just need to show up.

Let's look at what misconfiguration looks like for each persona.

The Individual

"I didn't know my doorbell had a login."

Yeah, well...it does.

And so does your smart fridge, your robot vacuum, and that "budget" Wi-Fi camera you got off Amazon with 12 five-star reviews and one horrifying backdoor.

Most people don't configure their devices. They:

- Plug them in
- Connect to Wi-Fi
- Download the app
- And never think about them again

Meanwhile, those devices:

- Never get updated
- Still have factory credentials
- Broadcast metadata
- Open ports like they're hosting a LAN party

Default isn't best...it's just the path of least resistance.

And guess who else loves low-effort targets? Literally every attacker, ever. The manufacturer just wants you to enjoy your connected toaster...they don't give a rat's ass about your security, let alone your 401K.

What To Fix (Yes, You Have To Log In):

And yes, some of this repeats... some nails don't go all the way in on the first hammer strike.

- Change default credentials:
  - Routers
  - Smart home devices (yes, ALL of them)
  - Security cameras
- Disable UPnP unless you know you need it (spoiler: you probably don't)
- Turn off remote admin access on home routers. Seriously, you don't need to fiddle with your router from Tonga.
- Update firmware regularly (yes, even your doorbell)
- Use guest network segmentation (from Chapter 1)

You bought convenience. But you inherited risk.

And if your devices are out there broadcasting open services, don't be surprised when someone connects.

Quick Wins for Individuals:

Task	Why It Matters	Tool/How-To
Change default device passwords	Prevents trivial takeover	Router/device web interfaces
Disable unnecessary features	Shrinks your attack surface	Router/device settings
Regularly update firmware	Patches known vulnerabilities	Router/device update menus

The Side-Hustler

"I used a website builder—it should be secure by default, right?"

Bless your heart... Not even close.

Website builders like Squarespace, Wix, and Shopify do a lot, but they don't protect you from:

- Misconfigured plugins
- Sloppy redirect rules
- Weak permissions
- Default admin pages

Plus, if you've spun up a WordPress site, installed 12 plugins from developers you found on Reddit, and skipped the SSL cert because "I'm just testing it," congratulations, you're hosting a ransomware honeypot.

What to Actually Do:

- Change your CMS admin URL (don't leave it as /admin or /wp-admin)
- Use a WAF like Cloudflare (even free tier is worth it)

- Remove unused plugins/themes...they're unpatched liabilities
- Lock down file permissions (hint: *777* is bad)
- Turn off directory listing on web servers

I know it's tedious... but please, for the love of uptime, sanity, and your customer's credit card numbers... check every, single, configuration and set it to its most secure setting unless you absolutely know why you'd do otherwise, and what risk that presents to you and your customers.

A side hustle is still a business. If it runs on a public-facing site, you owe it the 30 minutes it takes to not launch it with a wide-open config.

Quick Wins for Side-Hustlers:

Task	Why It Matters	Tool/How-To
Harden CMS/admin portals	Prevent brute-force attacks	WordPress hardening guides
Remove unused plugins/themes	Reduce attack surface	Admin ***UI (User Interface)*** + plugin security audits
Use a WAF	Filter common attacks before they hit you	Cloudflare free account

The Mid-Cap Boss

"We've got a standard image. Everything's secure."

Until someone bypasses the image. Or the image was built three years ago. Or someone cloned a prod ***VM (Virtual Machine)*** for testing and left it running...,with default admin creds intact.

Default configurations are everywhere. And in mid-sized companies, they often live where no one's looking:

- Cloud workloads without hardened templates
- Laptops that ship from vendors with bloatware and garbage firewall rules
- Internally-hosted apps using built-in root accounts
- Servers with ***SSH*** or RDP exposed to the internet "just for today"

Mid-Cap Moves:

- Build hardened gold images, and actually keep them updated to current patch levels.
- Use ***CIS Benchmarks*** to configure OSes, cloud services, and apps

- Scan configs with tools like:
    - Lynis (for Linux)
    - Microsoft Security Compliance Toolkit
    - ScoutSuite (for cloud)
    - GitGuardian, TruffleHog, or Whispers for credential leaks in code - because leaving AWS keys in GitHub is still somehow a thing
    - Nessus or OpenVAS for broad auditing
- Segment environments...prod doesn't talk to dev, and IoT doesn't belong anywhere near finance
- Log and alert on critical config changes

A "standard build" that nobody reviews isn't standard, it's outdated. And an outdated config is just a welcome mat for bad actors.

Quick Wins for Mid-Cap Bosses:

Task	Why It Matters	Tool/How-To
Hardened images + config scanning	Prevent misconfigurations	CIS Benchmarks + audit tools
Enforce environment segmentation	Contain breaches	Firewall rules, ***VPC (Virtual Private Cloud)*** segmentation
Monitor config drift	Detect bad changes early	***CSPM (Cloud Security Posture Management)*** tools, ***SIEM (Security Incident and Event Management)*** config alerts

The Enterprise Executive

"We have policies for that."

Sure you do. Now, show me:

- Who owns configuration standards?
- Are they enforced at deployment?
- Are they tested in staging?
- Are deviations logged, alerted, and remediated?

Because if not, your policy is just a dusty PDF no one reads, until legal, or an auditor demands to know who screwed up and why.

Worse: in many enterprises, systems are deployed via ***automated infrastructure***, but the underlying templates haven't been reviewed in years. ***IaC (Infrastructure as Code)*** is only secure if the **code itself is *hardened.***

What You Should Be Promoting:

- Baseline config policies...auto-enforced during deployment, not after
- Hardening at the Infrastructure-as-Code (IaC) level:

    - Terraform
    - Ansible
    - Puppet
- Continuous config drift detection (hello, CSPM tools)
- Executive-level dashboards:
    - % of assets meeting config baseline
    - Number of config drift events
    - % of cloud assets with insecure ports open
    - If any of the above go up, ask for an ***RCA (Root Cause Analysis)***
- Real accountability:
    - Configs tied to system owners
    - Violations tracked like real incidents

Secure configuration is table stakes. If your teams can't prove ***configuration hygiene***, they're not managing risk, they're just *hoping* the auditors don't know what Shodan is.

Quick Wins for Enterprise Execs:

Task	Why It Matters	Action
Enforce secure baselines	Stops drift before it starts	IaC templates + pre-deploy scans
Continuous monitoring	Catch config failures fast	CSPM tools + SIEM integration
Make config hygiene a leadership metric	Keep execs focused on real risk	Regular reporting on drift/exposure

Real-World Fails

- An engineer deployed a dev database (DB) to AWS with public access "for testing." It contained production data. Nobody noticed...until it got scraped by a bot and listed for sale.
- A company left Jenkins accessible on the public internet with no login required. It was used to drop ransomware across multiple build servers.
- A university's IoT HVAC system came pre-installed with Telnet enabled. That system later became part of a DDoS botnet.

Final Thought for Chapter 4

You can't secure what you deploy like it's 2004.

"Click-happy" installs are the silent killer of modern infrastructure.

Stop assuming defaults are safe and start making **secure** the default.

Quick Wins by Persona

Persona	Quick Win	Why It Matters	Tool/How-To
Individual	Change default passwords + disable remote admin	Prevents external takeover of home devices	Router UI, device apps
Side-Hustler	Harden CMS + use a WAF	Protects your storefront from drive-bys	Cloudflare, Sucuri, admin settings
Mid-Cap Boss	Build/maintain hardened images + scan configs	Avoids lazy deployment risk	CIS Benchmarks, Nessus, OpenVAS
Enterprise Exec	Monitor drift, enforce IaC hardening	Keeps cloud and infra secure at scale	CSPM tools, IaC linting, config dashboards

Chapter Five

No, Sharon Does NOT need Domain Admin

CIS Control 5—Account Management

Alternate Title:

"Cyber Criminals don't break in... They log in"

Opening Story: "He Hasn't Worked Here Since 2019"

It started with a help desk ticket:

"Can someone explain why a former employee account just logged in at 3am from Belarus?"

Turns out "Jake" had left the company four years ago. He was part of a small DevOps team...smart guy, built a few internal tools, ran some batch jobs. His access never got disabled.

Why?

Because:

- HR never closed the loop with IT
- The team still used one of his old automations
- And someone said, "Just leave it for now, we'll fix it later"

Fast forward to 2025. That account still had VPN access, admin creds in a Git repo, and elevated access to a Jenkins pipeline that deployed to prod.

An attacker found his credentials in an old breach. Tried them. They worked.

What followed:

- Full environment compromise
- Ransomware across prod and staging
- Customer data exposure
- A $1.7M ***incident response (IR)*** invoice

All because nobody cleaned up after "Jake."

Lesson:

Accounts are doorways.

If you don't close them when someone leaves, or if you leave the wrong ones wide open, it's not a question of *if* someone walks in...it's *when.*

BLUF (Bottom Line Up Front)

Every account is a doorway.

Some are wide open.

Some have no doorknob.

Some lead to the vault, and nobody remembers who built them.

If you don't know:

- Who has accounts
- What those accounts can do
- Whether they're still used
- And how they're monitored

...then congratulations: you're running an open-access theme park for attackers.

CIS Control 5 exists to help you track, manage, and kill off the accounts you forgot you had.

Because it's not always a zero-day that gets you, it's the marketing intern who still has admin rights in AWS.

The Individual

"It's just me—I don't have accounts to manage."

Oh really? Let's count:

- Your email
- Your banking logins
- Social media accounts
- Online shopping profiles (likely hundreds)
- App store accounts
- Cloud storage
- Utilities, insurance, travel

And how many of those use the same password?

How many are still active even though you haven't logged in for years?

And what happens if one of them gets breached? Can they use that to hop into your inbox, cloud storage, or bank account? (Thanks for that, "Sign in with Facebook.")

Fix Your Personal Account Chaos:

- Use a password manager (seriously, you're in Ch 5 now, and we covered this in Ch 1)
- Review saved logins in your browser, phone, apps, and kill what you don't need.
- Delete old accounts: Use sites like JustDelete.me and Mozilla Monitor
- Enable MFA on everything that matters (especially email, banking, cloud storage). You can also choose passkey or passwordless... anything is better than username/pw
- If you're not going to use a Password Manager, please at least use unique logins for sensitive services (bank ≠ email ≠ Netflix login)

Quick Win for Individuals:

Task	Why It Matters	Tool/How-To
Delete unused accounts + enable MFA	Reduces attack surface, stops reuse attacks	JustDelete.me + Authenticator apps

The Side-Hustler

"It's just me and maybe my VA (Virtual Assistant)—I don't need anything fancy."

Until your VA deletes your Stripe account, your designer uploads malware to your Shopify store, or your intern logs in from a Romanian café with free malware on tap.

Even a solo business needs access controls:

- Shared tools
- Client data
- Payment platforms
- Email marketing systems

Side-Hustler Account Hygiene:

- Create individual user accounts for every contractor, partner, assistant, etc. (No shared passwords/accounts!)
- Use ***role-based access*** where possible (Shopify staff accounts, Google Workspace roles)

- Revoke access immediately when the job ends (yes, even for your cousin, the graphic designer)
- Keep a master inventory of accounts + users, dates onboarded, dates offboarded and check it against current status regularly.
- Enable MFA across all services (storefronts, payment, email, etc.)

Also, don't allow guest accounts to be tied to public email domains (ie, Gmail, GMX, Proton, etc.). You want corporate emails so you can tie it to contractual relationships. Remember, if it has your name, your brand, or your money tied to it...it's worth securing.

Quick Win for Side-Hustlers:

Task	Why It Matters	Tool/How-To
Create separate accounts for VAs/tools	Tracks who did what, limits blast radius	Platform user management + MFA

The Mid-Cap Boss

"We have user accounts in Active Directory—what more do we need?"

Plenty. Like:

- **A process to kill accounts** when people leave or change roles
- **Regular access reviews** documented, recorded, audited
- **Unique accounts** for services and integrations
- **No more shared admin logins**
- **No lingering ex-employee accounts** tied to key systems

Account sprawl in mid-sized orgs is where things get dangerous:

- **Shadow accounts** tied to internal apps
- **Orphaned accounts** post-layoffs
- **Overprivileged roles** because “we didn’t have time to make a custom one”

Mid-Cap Controls to Implement:

- Centralize account management through ***SSO (Single Sign On)/IdP (Identity Provider)*** (Okta, MS EntraID, Google Workspace)
- Tie deprovisioning to HR offboarding processes (no termination is complete without access revocation)
- Run quarterly access reviews, especially privileged accounts
- Use service accounts with ***least privilege*** needed (no, your Jenkins bot doesn't need root, nor does it need to connect to 100 servers)
- Ban shared accounts: No more "ITAdmin01" with a sticky-note password. Assign real users and real roles, and have real audit trails.

In the world of access, reduce, reduce, reduce. If your intern has access to payroll, the problem isn't them...it's you.

Quick Win for Mid-Cap Bosses:

Task	Why It Matters	Tool/How-To
Centralize identity & enforce offboarding	Kills orphaned accounts, improves visibility	Okta, Azure AD, HR/IT integrations

The Enterprise Executive

"We have identity governance and privileged access workflows."

Fantastic. But:

- Are they actually enforced?
- Are they tested?
- Are they reported on?
- Are privileged accounts reviewed?
- Do you actually know how many you have... and how many also have ***Local Admin*** on their laptop, unsecured WiFi at home, and a 12-character password from 2020 that they also use for Steam?
- Is there real behavioral monitoring?

Here's the hard truth: **attackers love accounts more than exploits.** Why spend time finding/spending a zero-day when someone's over-provisioned their Box folder and forgot?

What You Should Be Driving:

- Roll out ***PAM (Privileged Access Management)*** tools

(CyberArk, BeyondTrust)

- Mandate federated identity and SSO enforcement
- Automate account lifecycle: onboarding to offboarding
- Conduct regular access certification audits (quarterly, if not more)
- Deploy behavioral analytics on account usage (not just login success/failure)

And yes, **you** need to do the phishing tests and implement MFA like everyone else.

Leadership isn't immunity, it's accountability, with visibility attached.

If your account gets popped, it's now both a headline...and a case study.

Quick Win for Enterprise Execs:

Task	Why It Matters	Tool/How-To
Enforce access reviews + push PAM	Prevents privilege creep and shadow accounts	CyberArk, BeyondTrust, identity governance suites

Real-World Fails

- An AWS account belonging to a former dev was never removed. It had full admin access. That account got compromised via GitHub credentials, and $300,000 in cloud spend got racked up mining crypto.
- A finance team used a shared Excel sheet with stored passwords for bank logins. A phishing email led to that file getting uploaded...and drained accounts.
- A former CMO's access to marketing automation was never revoked. Months later, it was used to send a phishing campaign to 40,000 customers of the company (not great for their reputation).

Final Thought for Chapter 5

You don't need a breach to be vulnerable.

You just need one forgotten account, one shared login, or one over-permissioned role.

Accounts are weapons in the wrong hands.

Make sure they're not yours...

Or the next breach headline might include your name and job title.

Quick Wins by Persona

Persona	Quick Win	Why It Matters	Tool/How-To
Individual	Delete unused accounts + use MFA	Reduces exposure across your digital life	JustDelete.me, password manager
Side-Hustler	Create separate accounts for VAs/tools	Tracks who did what, and limits blast radius	Platform user management + MFA
Mid-Cap Boss	Centralize identity & enforce offboarding	Kills orphaned accounts + improves visibility	Okta, Azure AD, HR/IT integration
Enterprise Exec	Enforce access reviews + push PAM	Prevents privilege creep and shadow accounts	CyberArk, BeyondTrust, governance tools

Chapter Six

MFA Isn't Optional—and No, You Can't Just Use SMS

CIS Control 6—Access Control Management

Alternate Title:

"You Don't Need Access... You Just Think You Do"

Opening Story: "But I Had MFA..."

It started with a text.

A Twilio employee received a simple phishing message:

"Your account has unusual activity. Please verify immediately."

It linked to a page that looked exactly like Twilio's login portal. Even the URL was spot on...except for a single Cyrillic character substitution.

The employee entered their credentials...and their MFA code.

The attacker, watching in real-time, immediately used it to log in, pulled session tokens, and pivoted into Okta support systems.

The result?

- Over 100 downstream companies compromised, including Signal, DoorDash, and Cloudflare
- Additional stolen session tokens leading to more hijacks
- A total damage bill likely in the hundreds of millions

The root issues?

- No phishing-resistant MFA
- No behavioral controls
- Over-permissioned accounts
- And blind trust in session tokens that could be hijacked

Lesson:

Having MFA isn't the same as having *secure* access.
If your MFA can be phished, fatigued, or bypassed, you're still wide open and you don't have control. You have a participation ribbon.

BLUF (Bottom Line Up Front)

Access control isn't about trust.
It's about **verifying, restricting, and monitoring**...relentlessly.

If you're not managing access by:

- Role
- Context
- Risk
- and Continuous verification

...then you're handing out backstage passes to anyone with a fake clipboard and a confident smile.

MFA isn't a cure-all...especially if:

- It's SMS-based (easy to hijack)
- It's fatigable (tap-to-approve spam)
- It's not enforced on **every** app, **every** time
- It's only on the login, not on key actions

CIS Control 6 isn't just about MFA.

It's about **who gets in, what they can do, and how long they can do it for.** Let's see how that plays out across our four favorite personas.

The Individual

"I turned on MFA—I'm good, right?"

Sure, you're better. But not bulletproof.

If your MFA is:

- SMS-based → vulnerable to SIM-swapping
- App-based → vulnerable to approval fatigue
- Email-based → tied to a compromised email account

Then you've still got major holes.

Personal Access Control Moves:

- **Use app-based MFA**, not SMS (Authy, Duo, Google Authenticator, 1Password, etc. Google has a great tutorial on how to install and use Google Auth)
- **Don't "approve" blindly:** If you didn't initiate the login, deny it and change your password immediately...you're in the middle of an attack
- **Enable notifications** for new logins or access requests for all of your important apps and accounts.

- **Review connected devices** and sessions regularly (Google, Apple, Amazon, etc.). If you have multiple sessions active, kill them all and start new.
- **Review *authentication* logs** from all your stuff...see where unsuccessful attempts are coming and the frequency...if it's consistently high, consider changing your email address.
- **Revoke old sessions and access tokens** by logging out (not just closing the browser) of every session you establish with an account...and clear your browser cache regularly.

If you're using SMS MFA, your security is only as strong as Chad at the Verizon kiosk who just got socially engineered into porting your number to Russia.

Quick Win for Individuals:

Task	Why It Matters	Tool/How-To
Switch to app-based or hardware MFA	Reduces SIM-swap and phishing risk	Authy, 1Password, YubiKey

The Side-Hustler

"I'm the only one logging in—it's fine."

Nope. Your risk comes from:

- OAuth app permissions
- API tokens
- VA's/contractors
- That same browser session you've had open since 2019
- Session hijacks from bad Wi-Fi

Your risk isn't just **who logs in;** it's **what gets authorized** behind the scenes. Most side-hustlers forget that OAuth permissions are **permanent until revoked**. That sketchy SEO tool you tested for a week? It might still have full access to your customer email list...and it doesn't even work anymore.

Side-Hustler Access Control:

- **Use hardware-based MFA** for anything money-related (YubiKey, Titan, etc.) Even software based (passkey) is preferable over username/password.

- **Separate business and personal logins:** Don't run your Etsy-shop and Netflix from the same browser profile
- **Audit OAuth apps** connected to Google, Facebook, and Shopify
- **Set up alerts** for new logins, password resets, or permissions changes

You don't need a team to have insider threats.
You just need one app integration gone rogue.

Quick Win for Side-Hustlers:

Task	Why It Matters	Tool/How-To
Audit app permissions + OAuth access	Prevents third-party hijack	Google/Facebook App Security Settings

The Mid-Cap Boss

"We enforce MFA, so we're good."

So... let's define "enforce."

- Every app, or just the SSO login?
- Every session?
- Every role?
- Is the MFA phishing-resistant, or just push-notifications?
- Is legacy authentication blocked?
- Is conditional access enabled, managed, and monitored?

Has anybody in your org used social-login for anything? Are they using personal Google accounts to authenticate business tools because it's "easier"? Have you audited the shadow app ecosystem connected to their identities?

Spoiler: if you're not blocking social logins and restricting OAuth scopes, **your org's data is flowing through endpoints you've never seen.**

Mid-Cap Access Controls That Matter:

- Use phishing-resistant MFA (***FIDO2*** tokens, push with number matching)
- Kill SMS MFA wherever possible
- Block social login connections (LinkedIn/Facebook/Google auth)
- Implement Conditional Access Policies:
    - Stronger auth for high-risk logins
    - Require reauth for sensitive operations
    - Block legacy authentication (***IMAP/POP***)
- Just-In-Time access for elevated privileges
- Log and review access requests, failed/successful logins, and role/privilege changes

Quick Win for Mid-Cap Bosses:

Task	Why It Matters	Tool/How-To
Implement Conditional Access + Just-In-Time	Prevents lateral movement and escalation	Azure Conditional Access, Duo, JumpCloud

The Enterprise Executive

"We have conditional access and federated identity. We're good."

Cool, so in addition to everything you just read in the Mid-Cap section... Let's check:

- How many users are exempt?
- How many apps are outside of SSO?
- How many admins have persistent elevated access?
- How fast is escalation if a risky login is detected?

Do your risk dashboards tell you *where*, *when*, and *why* high-risk logins occur? Or just that "MFA is turned on"? Has your ***SOC (Security Operations Center)*** built alerting that escalates with each additional risk factor? Are you adding rules as attack indicators change?

Executive Access Governance:

- Mandate phishing-resistant MFA org-wide (Start with C-Suite, Finance, and IT)
- Require re-authentication after privilege escalation

- Review all conditional access policies quarterly (and ask "is this still relevant?")
- Eliminate standing admin access: ***Time-bound elevation*** only
- Monitor risky sign-ins with behavioral analytics, and alert to the SOC
- Audit access exceptions...execs included (no more "Steve from Dev needs bypass because reasons")

And yes: check if your own account is using SMS MFA, has device registration issues, or is excluded from policy "because exec."

By the way, when was the last time someone ran an *actual* audit of your access exemptions?

If you're not willing to be treated like a threat actor during a red team engagement, you're not serious about leading a secure access culture.

CEOs don't get popped because of tools, they get popped because of exceptions.

A Word on Passwordless (Because I Hope You Were Going to Ask)

There's a lot of hype around *passwordless authentication*...and for good reason. FIDO2-based passkeys and device-bound credentials *can* reduce your exposure to phishing and credential stuffing. But don't mistake buzzwords for silver bullets.

Here's what works:

- **FIDO2-based logins (hardware or platform)**: Bound to your device, phishing-resistant
- **Device-native biometrics** (FaceID, Windows Hello): When backed by a strong underlying identity system

- **Passkeys**: When you're syncing through a trusted provider (Apple, Google, or Microsoft ecosystem)

Here's what doesn't:

- Just slapping "passwordless" on top of an OAuth app and calling it secure
- Using OTP codes sent via email (still phishable)
- Letting passwordless become a new excuse to skip re-authentication or monitoring

If you're going passwordless, do it right. It's not "less/more secure"; it's *differently secure*, and it still requires governance.

Quick Win for Enterprise Execs:

Task	Why It Matters	Tool/How-To
Eliminate standing admin + review exceptions	Removes easy wins for attackers	PAM tools, Identity Governance suites

Real-World Fails

- An executive exempt from MFA got phished and had their inbox scraped, leaking sensitive M&A docs. ***SEC (Security and Exchange Commission)*** was not thrilled, neither were shareholders.
- An MFA fatigue attack on a DevOps engineer allowed access to internal cloud infrastructure. Result: ransomware across prod and backups.
- A marketing app used OAuth to connect to G-Suite Gmail with full read/write. After a breach, it was used to send phishing campaigns from internal email addresses. Had to reset the entire IdP, apologize to countless other orgs, and do serious PR damage control.

Final Thought for Chapter 6

MFA isn't optional.

Strong access control isn't optional.

And your SSO portal isn't your magical shield.

You can't trust users.

You can't trust devices.

You can't even trust policy exceptions.

Lock it all down, or someone else will.

Quick Wins by Persona

Persona	Quick Win	Why It Matters	Tool/How-To
Individual	Switch to app-based or hardware MFA	Reduces risk of SIM swap and phishing	Authy, 1Password, YubiKey
Side-Hustler	Audit app permissions + OAuth access	Prevents third-party hijack or abuse	Google/Facebook App Security Settings
Mid-Cap Boss	Implement Conditional Access + Just-In-Time	Prevents lateral movement and escalation	Azure Conditional Access, Duo, JumpCloud
Enterprise Exec	Eliminate standing admin + review exemptions	Removes easy wins for attackers	PAM tools, Identity Governance Suites

Chapter Seven

Kill What You Don't Use

CIS Control 7—Continuous Vulnerability Management

Alternate Title:

"Zombie Servers and Forgotten Cloud Stuff Will Wreck You"

Opening Story: "It Was Just a Test Server..."

It wasn't supposed to be permanent.

A cloud engineer at a federally-regulated financial organization spun up a test VM in AWS to trial a new logging agent. Just a quick experiment. No big deal.

- No tag
- No expiration.
- No entry in the inventory

The config?

- Public I
- SSH enabled
- Default OS image (with three known ***CVEs (Common Vulnerabilities and Exposures)***)
- Root login via password

It sat idle... for months. Even finance didn't see a charge for it thanks to a free-tier credit.

Unmonitored.

Unpatched.

Unnoticed.

Until attackers found it with a basic public scan.

They Brute-forced the password, dropped a crypto miner application, and then pivoted to start scanning other organizations.

The financial org only discovered it after another company's SOC detected the outbound scans and reported it. One test box, no tags, and no lifecycle management.

The result? An active federal investigation, potential regulatory fines, and a serious black eye.

Lesson:

Spinning stuff up is easy.

Tracking its lifecycle and shutting it down is the discipline that saves you.

BLUF (Bottom Line Up Front)

If you don't actively kill what you don't use, it will become a liability.

CIS Control 7 exists because abandoned, unmanaged, or forgotten assets are among the **#1** entry points for attackers.

If you're not:

- Continuously discovering assets
- Continuously reviewing them
- Decommissioning what's not needed
- Automating lifecycle tagging
- Alerting on asset drift

...then you're basically letting attackers roam your IT leftovers. **Every asset you forget is an opportunity for someone else to remember.**

Let's fix it.

The Individual

"It's just my laptop. And maybe a smart speaker. And that old iPad in the drawer..."

Wrong (and yeah, this is gonna sound familiar).

Every smart TV, tablet, printer, phone, gaming console, connected IoT device, cloud account, and whatever random online services you don't even remember subscribing to is another open door if not properly managed.

Based on a 2024 NordPass survey, the average Joe in the US has somewhere around 168 passwords for personal use, and 87 work/business-related accounts. This number includes both active and dormant accounts, as many people forget to delete unused accounts (remember my advice back in Ch. 1 and 2?).

Americans lead globally in device ownership, with the number of connected devices per household and per person steadily rising:

In 2023, the average U.S. household had 17 connected devices (including smartphones, smart TVs, computers, tablets, and IoT/smart home devices).

Some sources report the number is even higher: as of 2023, the average U.S. household owned 21 connected devices across 13 device categories.

Regardless, I'm pretty confident you have WAY more than you think.

What You Should Do:

- **Make a personal asset list**: Start with your Wi-Fi network. What's connected? Then look at what's installed on each device (yes, software is an asset too).
- **Decommission what you don't use**: Wipe and recycle old devices, uninstall abandoned apps, cancel subscriptions you forgot about.
- **Check your cloud accounts**: Google Drive, Dropbox, iCloud. If you haven't touched it in 12 months, clean it up. **Digital hoarding is real...and exploitable.**
- **Secure your backups**: If it stores sensitive stuff, it needs encryption, cloud redundancy, and a plan. Carbonite, Google One, iCloud, Box...all support automated backups.

If you don't remember owning it, odds are it's not patched, not secure, and not necessary.

Quick Win for Individuals:

Task	Why It Matters	Tool/How-To
Scan your home network + cloud accounts	Find forgotten or risky stuff before attackers do	Fing App, Router UI, Google Security Center

The Side-Hustler

"I just run a few things online—how bad could it be?"

You're operating an unmanaged IT empire...let's take a peek:

- That dev server you spun up in 2020? Still online. Still vulnerable.
- That Firebase DB with public access? Leaking data.
- That unzipped site backup in your Gmail? A roadmap to your entire stack.
- That Virtual Server with Stripe test keys? Still reachable.

Welcome to your **shadow IT startup...**you just didn't file the paperwork.

Side-Hustler Cleanup Checklist:

- **Inventory your cloud services**: AWS, Azure, DigitalOcean, Firebase, Heroku, GitHub Pages, etc.
- **Kill what's not being used**: And don't just stop the VM...delete the account. Or it'll keep billing. Or leaking.
- **Tag everything**: Owner, purpose, last updated. Future-you will thank past-you.

- **Audit your domains**: Expired? Redirecting to old assets? Parked and misused? Own it or kill it.
- **Rotate your API keys**: And clean out old integrations you don't use anymore.

Your cloud footprint is likely *wider*, *older*, and *riskier* than you think.

Quick Win for Side-Hustlers:

Task	Why It Matters	Tool/How-To
Kill unused cloud assets + rotate keys	Prevent breach through abandoned junk	AWS console, GitHub, Firebase settings

The Mid-Cap Boss

"We do quarterly asset reviews... I think."

Cool. So does every company that ends up in a breach report.

Here's what mid-sized orgs love to do:

- Let business units spin up cloud resources with no governance
- Forget to decommission "temporary" test environments
- Assume tagging will happen magically (yes, you can automate it, but you must **enforce** it too)
- Rely on outdated spreadsheets and manual updates

That's not asset management. That's asset *guessing*.

Mid-Cap Controls to Implement:

- **Deploy automated discovery tools**: Rumble, Lansweeper, AWS Config, Azure Resource Graph.
- **Tag everything, or block it**: Owner, environment (dev/test/prod), data sensitivity, expiration date.
- **Set expiration alerts**: If it hasn't checked in for 30+ days, it needs

a review.

- **Tie your CMDB to provisioning**: No asset enters production without showing up in inventory.
- **Build a formal retirement process**: If a project ends, clean house. No "we might need it later" exceptions.

Dev environments are like zombies: **Kill them twice. Burn the body. Salt the earth.**

Quick Win for Mid-Cap Bosses:

Task	Why It Matters	Tool/How-To
Automate discovery + tag enforcement	Kill shadow IT before it kills you	Rumble, Lansweeper, AWS Config

The Enterprise Executive

"We have full CMDB coverage."

Do you? Really?

How about:

- Ephemeral cloud workloads and their images?
- Shadow SaaS apps?
- Employee home devices syncing corp data?
- Vendor-deployed "temporary" systems?

Your CMDB is only as good as the **real-time reconciliation behind it**. And if it's not backed by automation, it's just a dashboard-shaped lie.

What You Should Be Driving:

- **Are cloud assets tied to a real human?** (Every resource needs a named owner.)
- **Are we tracking ephemeral assets?** (Containers, spot instances, sandbox VMs.)
- **What's our discovery cadence?** (If it's not continuous, it's broken.)

- **Are we alerting on drift?** (Assets that move out of expected zones, configs, or policies.)

- **Do we enforce decommissioning?** (What's the sign-off flow? Who owns retirement?)

And yes...**check every cloud account you have access to.**

I'd bet money there's $10k+ in monthly spend on zombie infrastructure across dev, staging, and legacy sandboxes.

A few other fun items to consider:

- Data ownership tagging: You can't track risk if you can't track data.

- Automatic deprovisioning: Kill assets at project end, not "someday."

- M&A asset auditing: Shadow assets from acquisitions can sink you.

Quick Win for Enterprise Execs:

Task	Why It Matters	Tool/How-To
Audit CMDB drift + define asset lifecycle	Kill ghost systems before they haunt you	CMDB integrations, ***ITSM (IT Service Management)*** workflows

Real-World Fails

- A "temporary" Kubernetes cluster was never decommissioned. Access was wide open, and never changed. Displayed on Shodan, and ended up launching a DDoS attack, on its own company.
- A forgotten VM running out-of-date ***PHP*** led to internal database breaches, GDPR fines, and expensive damage control.
- A terminated employee's laptop was never recovered, and remained authenticated to VPN for months, was resold on eBay...and was still authenticated. The purchaser was honest, and reported it... the alternative would have been epic.

Final Thought for Chapter 7

If you don't track it, you can't patch it.

If you don't own it, you can't fix it.

If you can't shut it down, someone else will use it against you.

Treat "retirement" as part of asset management, not an afterthought.

Burn the zombies.

Quick Wins by Persona

Persona	Quick Win	Why It Matters	Tool/How-To
Individual	Scan home network + cloud accounts	Know what you actually own	Fing App, router UI, Google/Apple settings
Side-Hustler	Kill unused cloud assets + rotate keys	Prevent forgotten services from becoming threats	Cloud dashboards, GitHub, Firebase
Mid-Cap Boss	Automate discovery + enforce tagging	Real-time visibility with accountability	Rumble, AWS Config, Lansweeper
Enterprise Exec	Audit CMDB drift + define lifecycle policies	Eliminate ghost assets and stale systems	CMDB integrations, ITSM + cloud tooling

Chapter Eight

Patch the Damn Thing, or Make Peace with the Ransom Note

CIS Control 10—Malware Defenses & CIS Control 7—Continuous Vulnerability Management

Alternate Title:

"Congratulations, You're a Known Exploit!"

Opening Story: "The CVE Was Known—So Was the Outcome"

In March 2017, Apache Struts (a popular web application framework) disclosed a critical vulnerability: **CVE-2017-5638**. It allowed remote code execution through a malicious Content-Type header. Exploitable. Documented. Patched.

Equifax was running Apache Struts.

The vulnerability was flagged internally.

Patching guidance was sent to IT teams.

A fix was available.

And still, **months later**, one of Equifax's public-facing applications remained unpatched.

Attackers found the system, exploited the flaw, and began siphoning off **names, Social Security numbers, birthdates, driver's licenses, mortgage and credit card details;** the crown jewels of American identity.

147 million people were affected.

The cost?

- Over **$700 million** in settlements and legal penalties
- A **shattered reputation** and public trust
- **New SEC rules** on cyber disclosures
- And congressional hearings that dragged their entire C-suite into the hot seat

Shortly after the breach became public:

- The **CEO resigned**
- The **Chief Security Officer "retired"**
- The **CIO followed**

Not because they wrote bad code.

Not because they didn't have scanners.

But because **they failed to patch a known vulnerability**.

Lesson:

It wasn't a zero-day.

It wasn't a sophisticated nation-state attack.

It was a known bug and a missing patch.

And most importantly, it was a leadership fail.

BLUF (Bottom Line Up Front)

Patching isn't sexy.

It's not glamorous.

But it's how a huge percentage of real-world breaches could have been stopped.

Vulnerability management isn't just scanning and logging CVEs.

It's:

- Finding what's broken
- Prioritizing what matters
- Getting it fixed
- And making extremely sure it stays fixed

If your vuln management program doesn't **assign ownership**, **prioritize risk, enforce timelines**, and **close the loop**, you're not managing risk, you're just printing long PDF reports nobody reads.

And here's the kicker:

Most exploited vulnerabilities are **known** vulnerabilities.

The attackers didn't find them first. **You did.** You just didn't do anything about it.

Let's break it down by persona.

The Individual

"Patching? I just let my phone do its thing."

Except when it doesn't.

And except for your Wi-Fi router.

And your printer (more than once I've conducted vulnerability assessments on execs, and found my way onto a home network via a printer's web UI).

And your old Android tablet.

And your laptop that hasn't rebooted in a year...spoiler: It has to restart to apply all the updates.

Attackers love your personal network, because it's full of devices you forgot existed, and none of them are patched. As called out several times in previous chapters...put all the IoT (and your house guests) on a separate network.

What You Should Do:

- **Turn on automatic updates**: For your OS, browser, and apps. Stop hitting "Remind Me Tomorrow." Don't live in fear of that one time ten years ago that iPhones got bricked from an update.

- **Reboot once a week**: Yes, really. It installs the patches you've been "getting around to."

- **Update IoT devices manually**: Doorbells, TVs, routers, baby monitors...all need firmware checks (via app or web UI).
- **Replace unsupported gear**: If it hasn't had an update in years, it's now just a liability with a power cord.

If you're running unpatched gear at home, you're a test environment for attackers. And they don't need permission.

Honestly, this is one of the most commonly neglected parts of your cyber footprint, and it's so easy to keep up with...just do the thing!

Quick Win for Individuals:

Task	Why It Matters	Tool/How-To
Turn on auto-updates + reboot weekly	Actually installs critical patches	OS settings, router apps

The Side-Hustler

"It's just a little site—I'm not a target."

You keep using that excuse, and every botnet in the world disagrees.

Botnets scan the entire internet, including the IP associated with your website.

- You're running WordPress? Cool...so are 43% of websites. Guess where attackers focus.

- You've got old plugins or themes installed "just in case"? You've got new plugins you just found? They're all vulnerable.

- Your dev server hasn't been logged into since your Etsy banner redesign? Bet it's got **CVEs** that desperately need patching.

Side-Hustle Patch Plan:

- Run vulnerability scans: WPScan (WordPress), OWASP ZAP, Sucuri SiteCheck, Mozilla Observatory.

- Update CMS, plugins, themes immediately upon update availability.

- Remove old plugins/themes: Everything old is an attack vector.

- Use Dependabot or similar to patch app dependencies automatically.
- Patch your dependencies. If you host your own app, use tools like npm audit, pip-audit, or dependabot.
- Patch your payment systems and store integrations too (Stripe, PayPal extensions).

Small businesses get hit because they're unpatched and easy...not because they're high value. And the attackers just automate and run a volume business at your expense.

Quick Win for Side-Hustlers:

Task	Why It Matters	Tool/How-To
Scan and update Site/CMS/plugins/dependencies	Close the most common breach vectors	WPScan, ZAP, Sucuri, Dependabot

The Mid-Cap Boss

"We scan regularly. We're good."

Let's play a game called **"Show Me the Patch."**

You've got tools...great.

You've got scan results...awesome.

But unless:

- Findings are prioritized and assigned by risk, not just ***CVSS (Common Vulnerability Scoring System)*** number
- Work is assigned and tracked
- Status is reviewed
- And remediation is verified

...you've got **vuln theater**, not vuln management.

Also, monthly scans won't cut it. Move toward ***continuous assessment*** or, at minimum, **weekly cycles**.

Mid-Cap Vuln Management That Works:

- **Centralized infrastructure scanning**: Nessus, Qualys, Rapid7, OpenVAS, etc.
- **Patch orchestration**: Use WSUS, PDQ Deploy, or MDM tools

for endpoints.

- **Ticketing workflows**: Auto-create and assign Jira/ServiceNow ***tickets*** with ***SLAs (Service Level Agreements)*** based on severity.
- **Track to closure**: Don't mark it "resolved" until it's **validated** as fixed. Don't just trust the dev who *says* it's fixed...*verify it.*
- **Prioritize by risk, not CVSS**: Use environmental scoring (asset exposure, data sensitivity, exploitability).
- **Scan code and containers**: Include SAST/DAST (e.g., SonarQube, Veracode,/ZAP, Burp), container scans (Trivy, Grype), and secrets detection (GitLeaks, TruffleHog). Don't forget deprecated runtimes in places like AWS Lambda... bad guys love old versions of Node.

You might find yourself paralyzed with the volume of findings...this is where ***risk evaluation*** and ranking come in. The lower-risk stuff is still there, and still important, but some of that will need to be accepted until you cover all the high-risk issues. Risk acceptance is valid. Risk ignorance is negligence. Know the difference and document the hell out of it.

And remember:

A 10/10 vuln in a dev box behind a firewall? Less urgent.

A 7.5 vuln on an internet-facing critical asset with no WAF? **Fix it yesterday.**

Quick Wins for Mid-Cap Bosses:

Task	Why It Matters	Tool/How-To
Tie scan results to ticketing with SLAs	Forces visibility and accountability	Qualys → Jira, Nessus → ServiceNow
Create and maintain a Risk Register	Tracks unremediated risk, and allows you to track increased/decreased risk over time	Start with a spreadsheet: Risk Name, Risk Rank (based on likelihood and financial impact), and Date Identified. Tools can come later.

The Enterprise Executive

"We have a red team and a bug bounty program."

Having researchers find issues is great.

Not fixing them is criminal negligence and the SEC can put you in jail.

Ask yourself:

- Do you know how long it takes to close a ***P1 finding***?
- Who owns remediation for red team findings?
- Are bug bounty submissions tracked to closure, or do they get lost in Slack threads?
- Do you report on **mean time to remediate (MTTR)** at the leadership level?
- Do you have an up-to-date risk register that tracks languishing vulns, and have you seen it?

Vuln management doesn't end with reporting. It ends with resolution. Close the vuln, not just the Jira ticket.

What You Should Be Driving:

- **Governance over vulnerability intake**: Red teams, bug bounty, scanners, pen tests...all must feed into a **single** tracking system.
- **Remediation SLAs**: Timeframes for critical, high, and medium risk, enforced and escalated if missed...and 6 months for critical is not a defensible SLA
- **Ownership accountability**: Every vuln has a name next to it. And it's not "Security." It's the person or team with hands-on-keyboard who can fix it.
- **Executive reporting**: Include:
    - Top open vulns by business RISK, reflected in potential monetary loss
    - Aging tickets by system owner
    - % of criticals fixed in SLA vs exceeding SLA
- **Post-remediation validation**: Just because the ticket's closed doesn't mean the vuln is gone. Confirm. Test. Report.

You Don't Need to Patch Everything immediately... Just the Stuff That'll Wreck You

- Focus on exploitability + exposure
- Align with MITRE ATT&CK to know likely attack paths
- Use asset criticality tags to prioritize
- Track time-to-fix *and* time-to-discover

Again, you don't have to patch everything... But you better be patching the stuff that matters; **on purpose, with evidence, and with urgency.** This is about strategic risk reduction, not busywork.

Quick Win for Enterprise Execs:

Task	Why It Matters	Tool/How-To
Govern vuln intake + track MTTR org-wide	Proves risk reduction to board and auditors	Risk dashboards, governance tooling

Real-World Fails

- **Equifax** ignored a known vuln and lost 147M records.
- A fintech startup ignored dev server patches. Cost: $2.5M in ransom and recovery.
- A SaaS company ignored a bug bounty report for 11 months...got breached the week before they finally reviewed it.

As an Executive, beware the perverse incentive. If you're rewarding quick-turn, fast-release to production without simultaneously holding those same teams responsible for security issues found in production that need patching, **YOU** are the problem.

Final Thought for Chapter 8

The difference between a vulnerability and a breach?

About 90 days of inaction.

Patch what matters.

Kill the noise.

And never be the subject of a congressional hearing if you can avoid it.

Quick Wins by Persona

Persona	Quick Win	Why It Matters	Tool/How-To
Individual	Turn on auto-updates + reboot weekly	Patching only works if it gets installed	OS settings, browser/app update preferences
Side-Hustler	Scan and update CMS/plugins/deps	Prevent easy web-based exploits	WPScan, Sucuri, Dependabot
Mid-Cap Boss	Tie scan results to ticketing with SLA	Drives accountability	Qualys → Jira, Nessus → ServiceNow
Enterprise Exec	Govern vuln intake + track MTTR org-wide	Fix the right issues, fast	Risk dashboards, governance tooling

Chapter Nine

If It's Not Logged, It Didn't Happen

CIS Control 8—Audit Log Management

Alternate Title:

"You Can't Investigate What You Didn't Bother to Record"

Opening Story: "Who Was In The Vault?"

A finance company suffered a major breach.

Sensitive client data disappeared.

They knew **something** had happened...

But when investigators asked for access logs, the company discovered a little problem:

- Firewall logs? Rotated every 7 days.
- VPN logs? Missing entirely.

- Admin account logins? Only last week's were saved.
- Endpoint detection logs? Disabled "to save space."

The verdict?

They had **no evidence** to show how the breach happened...or even what had been accessed.

In other words:

They couldn't prove how the attacker got in. They couldn't show how far the attackers went. They couldn't even determine when it started.

Their regulators *loved* that.

So did their customers' lawyers.

SEC Fines, ***GLBA*** enforcement, and years of litigation.

Lesson:

Logging is the black box of your digital environment.

No logs? No answers. No mercy.

BLUF (Bottom Line Up Front)

Audit logs are your black box recorder.

They tell you:

- What happened
- Who did it
- When it happened
- From where

- And (if you're lucky) how

Without proper logging, you're blind during incidents, mute during audits, and utterly screwed during litigation.

And yet...

- Logs are often incomplete
- Misconfigured
- Stored in the wrong place
- Or worse: not even turned on

If your logs don't exist, don't persist, or don't correlate, then you don't have log management, you have *log-flavored regret.*

And during a breach, that's the difference between "incident contained" and "class action lawsuit incoming."

Let's break it down by persona.

The Individual

"Wait... my home stuff has logs?"

Yes, but don't feel bad for not knowing. Everything from your laptop to your smart toaster is logging something.

And while you may not need enterprise-grade SIEM tooling at home, **basic visibility** is still part of *not sucking at cybersecurity.*

What You Can (and Should) Do:

- **Check login activity**: Google, Apple, Microsoft, Amazon all let you see past logins. Review them. Regularly. You'll see if someone is poking at your login pages. If they are, take defensive action:
  - Change passwords. Longer is better.
  - Ensure MFA is enabled (to an authenticator app like Google Authenticator, not just an SMS prompt).
- **Router logs**: Most home routers log connections. Peek at who's showing up on your network. Same story here...if someone is pounding on your router, or worse yet, is connected to it, take action:
  - Change the admin password

    - Change the login password
    - Reset all connections

- **Firewall logs:** OK, so maybe you don't have a Firewall (or know what one is). Odds are, you have firewall settings on your Router if you don't have a specific hardware Firewall. You also likely have software firewalls on your laptop.
    - Confirm admin and login passwords are changed to your own, secure passwords
    - Block all incoming traffic except for specific ports that are required for your applications and services
    - Allow outbound traffic for only the devices on your network that need access to the internet
    - Enable logging for firewall events to monitor and analyze network activity
- **Cloud storage activity logs**: Dropbox, iCloud, Google Drive show file access history that can help spot shady changes or rogue shares. And clean up old shares...Bob doesn't need access to that folder from 2019.
- **Email activity**: Look for forwarding rules you didn't set, or login locations that don't match your time-zone. If you're not actively using forwarding, disable it.

You don't need to be a SIEM wizard. Just aware enough to spot the weird...and stop it.

Quick Win for Individuals:

Task	Why It Matters	Tool/How-To
Check login activity + router logs	Spot suspicious access early	Account security pages, router admin panels

The Side-Hustler

"My web host handles security, right?"

Maybe. Maybe not. And are you checking?

Because when your store gets popped, Stripe and PayPal are going to ask **you** for evidence...not your host.

So, can you:

- Access your logs?
- Search them?
- Tell who logged in, from where, and when?
- Prove a suspicious transaction was fraudulent or user error?

And all that stuff in the "Individual" category above? That applies. Even more so. Your personal stuff is a potential gateway into your side-hustle.

Side-Hustle Log Hygiene:

- **Enable access logs**: In cPanel, WordPress, or whatever platform you use. Store them *off the web root*. Ideally, store them in a separate, immutable cloud store (Carbonite, Google backup, etc)
- **Use a plugin** (WordPress, Squarespace, Shopify) that logs admin

activity. And keep it updated. Always.

- **Monitor for logins and changes**: Services like Cloudflare, Sucuri, or Jetpack (for WordPress) can alert you to logins, file changes, or brute-force attacks. Cloudflare free tier is gold.
- **Set log retention**: Don't let logs rotate every 7 days. Aim for 30–90 days at minimum. You likely won't know something bad is happening until weeks after the initial pop.

If your whole business lives online, logs are your last line of defense when the lights flicker.

Quick Win for Side-Hustlers:

Task	Why It Matters	Tool/How-To
Enable and store site access logs securely	Prove integrity or detect compromise	Web host control panel, CMS plugins

The Mid-Cap Boss

"We have a logging server...somewhere."

That's adorable. When's the last time someone reviewed those logs? Can those logs be changed/deleted by an attacker?

Also, do you know:

- What's being logged?
- Where it's going?
- Who has access?
- How long it's stored?
- And whether **anyone** is actually processing and analyzing those logs for indicators of compromise?

Mid-sized orgs love to deploy a "log solution" and call it a day...no parsing, no alerting, no analysis.

Mid-Cap Logging Done Right:

- **Centralize logs**: Ship everything to a SIEM (Splunk, LogRhythm, Sentinel, Wazuh, AlienVault, etc.) or logging backend (ELK, Graylog).

- **Standardize log formats**: JSON > plaintext. Timestamps > "sometime last Thursday." Oh, and ensure it timestamps to at least to the microsecond. A lot can happen in a tenth of a second, and correlation is hell without greater precision.
- **Enable logs for:**
    - Authentication attempts (success/fail)
    - Privileged actions (account creation, user privilege escalation, root/sudo, etc.)
    - Firewall/router activity
    - Application error logs
    - Admin panel access
- **Protect log integrity**: Use write-once storage or version-controlled buckets. Bad guys love to delete or alter logs on their way out.
- **Define retention**: At least 90 days for security events. More for regulated data environments (and in these environments, you need to ensure the logs aren't filled with sensitive data).
- **Alerting**: Don't just store logs. Alert on them...using automation (humans can't reasonably review 10,000 events, let alone 100,000,000). Then act on them. 404s are boring. Multiple failed logins on a Sunday night? Not boring.

Logs you never look at aren't security...they're clutter

Quick Win for Mid-Cap Bosses:

Task	Why It Matters	Tool/How-To
Centralize + alert on key events	Turns logs into usable early warning systems	ELK stack, Wazuh, AlienVault, MS-Sentinel

The Enterprise Executive

"We have a SIEM and quarterly compliance audits...we're good."

First part, ok. "We're good"...maybe not. All of the content preceding this section applies as usual, and...

Do your logs:

- Correlate across systems?
- Flag anomalies based on baselines?
- Support eDiscovery and litigation?
- Satisfy your data residency and regulatory requirements?

And here's the spicy one:

When was the last time you personally saw a logging metrics dashboard?

You're the boss, you need to ask the right questions.

Executive Moves That Matter:

- **Log governance**: Define what *must* be logged, where it's stored, who owns it, and how it's protected. And for how long... Storage is cheap. Lawsuits aren't. Keep the logs.

- **Audit logs for your cloud infra and SaaS**: AWS CloudTrail, GCP Audit Logs, M365 unified audit logs, Okta system logs...**enable them.**
- **Centralized log correlation**: SIEM should tie together endpoint, network, auth, and app events, time-stamped to the microsecond. Granularity is king.
- **Alerting policies**: Define high-risk behavior signatures:
    - Impossible travel
    - Lateral movement
    - Off-hours privilege use
    - If you have UBEA, leverage it
- **Compliance-ready retention**:
    - PCI-DSS: 1 year
    - HIPAA: 6 years
    - SOX/GLBA: 7 years (in most cases)

Think through conflicting regulations, and how you'll justify it (GDPR, ***CCPA***, ***PIPL***, etc.)
Retention isn't just about compliance, it's about having answers when regulators, lawyers, or your board Chairman comes knocking six months after the fact.

- **Test incident response with log dependency**: Run a tabletop that *requires* pulling logs. As questions like "which specific customer accounts were compromised, and how much data was exfiltrated". Watch the panic in the system admin's face.

You're not paying for logging.
You're paying for answers *when everything goes wrong.*

Quick Win for Enterprise Execs:

Task	Why It Matters	Tool/How-To
Drive full-spectrum logging + actionable reporting	Detect breaches early and contain fast	SIEM + XDR + IR drills

Real-World Fails

- A ransomware group exploited a VPN credential, but because logs were only retained for 7 days, the entry point was never confirmed.
- A law firm couldn't prove data was or wasn't exfiltrated in a breach because file access logs weren't enabled. They lost clients anyway.
- An accounting firm suddenly started receiving rejected filings from the IRS... those clients had already filed their taxes. Except they hadn't. Someone had jumped in the middle, pulled the filing documents and credentials. The firm had zero logging, and zero answers. The IRS engaged and ruined their day.
- A cloud compromise in GCP went unnoticed for two weeks because Cloud Audit Logs were never turned on, and billing alerts were ignored.

Final Thought for Chapter 9

No logs = No forensics.

No forensics = No defense.

No defense = Full liability.

Log early. Log often. Log smart.

Quick Wins by Persona

Persona	Quick Win	Why It Matters	Tool/How-To
Individual	Check login activity + router logs	Spot suspicious access to your accounts/devices	Google/Apple login history, router web UI
Side-Hustler	Enable logs on sites + monitor login changes	Proves integrity when fraud or breach happens	Cloudflare, Sucuri, WP plugins
Mid-Cap Boss	Centralize + alert on key events	Turns logs into action	ELK, Wazuh, Sentinel, Rapid7 InsightIDR
Enterprise Exec	Drive governance + test log dependency	Validates security, legal, and compliance needs	SIEM + IR tabletop + unified audit framework

Chapter Ten

Email and Browsers... Your Gateways to Hell

CIS Control 9—Email and Web Browser Protections

Alternate Title:

"Your Inbox Is a War Zone and Chrome Is Basically Satan's Portal"

Opening Story: "One Click, Six Figures Gone"

The email looked legit.

- Perfect company logo
- Proper formatting
- A domain that resolved to the real vendor

An accounts payable employee (with local Admin) opened the invoice. Nothing weird. No error. No malware alert. Just a blank PDF.

No big deal, right?

Thirty minutes later:

- The PDF had launched a script which disabled EDR
- The attacker had moved laterally through the network
- Landed on the CFO's email account
- Exfiltrated sensitive contracts, and found a juicy one about to renew
- Registered a lookalike domain
- And requested a real wire transfer request for the renewal to a new bank account

$100,000+ was wired before anyone caught it.

Root causes?

- The email filter didn't catch the phish.
- The PDF payload didn't trigger any alerts because it used native commands.
- Local Admin rights allowed EDR to be disabled.
- And, nobody in finance received training to pause and verify financial requests before executing.

Lesson:

If phishing is the front door, your browser is the side window propped open with malware.

BLUF (Bottom Line Up Front)

Email and web browsers are the digital sidewalks where attackers hang out with signs that say 'Salma Hayek Leaves Nothing to the Imagination!', 'Elon Musk's Secret AI Scandal Revealed!' and 'Click Here for Invoices.'

They don't break in...they wait for you to *invite* them in.

If you're not:

- Filtering email content and attachments (turn on email security in M365/GCP)
- Hardening browser settings and extensions (set browsers to the highest security)
- Training users to pause before clicking (or don't click, in the case of Salma headlines)
- And watching for what slips through

...then you've handed over the keys and left a trail of snacks straight to your vault.

CIS Control 9 exists because phishing and drive-by attacks *still* work better than anything else. Why exploit a zero-day when you'll click a fake PDF and run the malware for them?

Let's break it down by persona.

The Individual

"Gmail has spam filters. I'm good, right?"

Cute. But attackers aren't hacking Gmail.

They're hacking **you**.

They just need you to click *that* link (or call that number).

The one pretending to be Amazon, Apple, or the IRS.

So despite the fact that your browsers and email clients do their best to filter that stuff out, the bad-guys always figure out ways around the defenses by convincing *you* to take action.

What You Should Do:

- **Use a modern browser** (Chrome, Firefox, Safari, Brave) and **keep it updated**
- **Turn on safe browsing** features (Google Safe Browsing, etc.)
- **Enable Gmail security features** like:
  - External sender warnings
  - Suspicious link detection
- **Don't install weird browser extensions**—and review what

you already have (ChromeLoader, Netflix Party, friGate, etc. Use VirusTotal to check out extensions)

- **Use an *ad blocker*** (uBlock Origin is a solid start). It stops malicious ads, not just annoying ones.
- **Preview links before clicking** (hover and check the URL)

And if your browser screams, *"Are you sure you want to visit this site?"* Don't feel like you're smarter than it. You're not. Hit "go back," pour a drink, and thank the engineers who saved your butt.

Quick Win for Individuals:

Task	Why It Matters	Tool/How-To
Enable Safe Browsing + Inspect URLs	Spot shady links before you click	Browser settings, link hovering

The Side-Hustler

"My web host scans my site for malware."

Sure. But if someone phishes your admin login, game over.

And you're responsible when your store starts redirecting to malware sites.

Oh, and that contact form that keeps getting spammed? That's not just spam...it's recon.

The same email address you use for customer support is now being used in phishing attempts, fake vendor outreach, and credential stuffing scams.

Also, if your email gets owned, they get:

- Your Stripe account
- Your customer conversations
- Your web admin reset links
- Your domain registrar
- Basically...everything

Lock It Down:

- **Use a separate email domain** for admin access (e.g., not support@yourshop.com)

- **MFA everything**...including your email client
- **Use *SPF*, *DKIM*, and *DMARC*** to prevent spoofing from your domain (Google and Mailchimp have good guides)
- **Disable HTML rendering in email** if your client allows it (makes malware harder to execute silently)
- **Use a secure contact form plugin** that strips scripts and sanitizes inputs
- **Route public email through a service with malware/virus scanning** (Google Workspace, Microsoft 365, ProtonMail, etc.)

If someone owns your inbox, they don't just own your business, they own your reputation, your revenue, and your customer list.

Quick Win for Side-Hustlers:

Task	Why It Matters	Tool/How-To
Use protected admin access + email filtering	Prevent account takeover or site hijack	Domain registrar, email security settings

The Mid-Cap Boss

"We have an email gateway. It's all good."

Hope is not a strategy.

And neither is trusting a single layer of defense.

Now that you have an email gateway, tell me:

- Are they ***sandboxing*** attachments?
- Are they filtering for credential phishing?
- Can they detect QR code-based phishing?
- How about Cyrillic, zero point, or other characters?
- And, do you have a business process to verify financial requests?

There's a wide variety of "email security" tools, and all are not equivalent. Some are in-line (Mimecast, Proofpoint), delay delivery while evaluation takes place, and require you to manage email through their interface, which may not match your native Outlook or Gmail experience...and definitely won't match your users' expectations. Some hook a copy of the email ***out-of-band***, and after evaluation, if they find a weaponized email, they pull it out of your inbox after the fact.

In either case, efficacy, delays, and user friendliness vary widely. And as attackers pivot to defeat defenses, your fancy email gateway is only as good as your people's worst click.

Mid-Cap Moves:

- **Use advanced email security tools** (Proofpoint, Mimecast, Microsoft Defender, Abnormal, Avanan)
- **Implement DKIM/SPF/DMARC** properly and monitor alignment failures
- **Run regular phishing simulations** (Gophish, KnowBe4, or Microsoft Attack Simulator)
- **Segment user roles for browser control policies**
    - Limit extensions
    - Disable macros in Office apps (Really. You have like three users who *actually* need macros...and two of them retire this year.)
- **Block access to known-bad domains via *DNS filtering*** (Quad9, Cisco Umbrella, Cloudflare Gateway)
- **Educate teams** on "lookalike" domains (rnicrosoft.com vs microsoft.com)

Also: build in the business process guardrails.

No single person should be able to approve a vendor payment on a Friday at 4:58 PM just because the CFO "slacked them."

Quick Win for Mid-Cap Bosses:

Task	Why It Matters	Tool/How-To
Layer email scanning + DNS/web filtering + simulations	Stop phishing and drive behavior change	Mimecast, Proofpoint, KnowBe4, Quad9, Cloudflare Gateway

The Enterprise Executive

"We have SEG, SOAR, XDR, and ZTNA."

Awesome. Huge wins...

Now let's ask:

- How many people are exempt from phishing simulations?
- Do browser logs integrate with your SIEM?
- Can your IR team trace a malicious email's full path, from delivery to click to execution?

Big orgs often have the tools... but lose the plot when it comes to **visibility**, **exceptions**, and **actual enforcement**. And staffing. If you don't have the FTE count to support a tool, you don't have a tool.

Having fancy acronyms doesn't mean your humans are protected.

What You Should Be Driving:

- **Email filtering + attachment sandboxing** org-wide, no exceptions
- **Shadow IT browser extension auditing** (via Chrome Enterprise, JAMF, or MDM)

- **Browser isolation** for high-risk roles or click-happy departments
- **Centralized DNS filtering + cloud proxy logging** for web access
- **Routine *BEC (Business Email Compromise)* tabletop exercises**
- **Tiered email security policies**: Executives, Finance, and HR should have *stricter* controls, not looser ones

Also, ask for a report of:

- Most-clicked phishing emails
- Most active risky domains
- Most abused browser plugins

And if your own email address is excluded from filtering "because VIP"...fix that *yesterday*.

Quick Win for Enterprise Execs:

Task	Why It Matters	Tool/How-To
Extend Zero Trust into browser/email access	Shrinks attacker options even after compromise	Browser isolation, strong DNS, XDR integrations

Real-World Fails

- **The "Make it stop beeping" fraud:** A senior citizen living in assisted living clicked on "something". The computer splashed up a pop-up and an urgent beeping came from the speakers. The splash screen said he'd been compromised, and he needed to call Microsoft Support at the listed number. He did. He downloaded the "support app", and the beeping stopped. An hour later, he'd gone to his credit union, withdrawn $24,000 in cash, and was trying to hail the transportation service to take him to meet a "remote bank manager" to "save his bank account".

- **A six-figure BEC (Business Email Compromise):** An attacker spoofed a vendor domain and sent a real-looking invoice to Accounts Payable. The invoice matched a contract that was actively renewing, right down to the amounts and terms. The only thing that didn't match? The bank account number. Nobody called to confirm. Nobody checked the sender domain closely. $475,000 gone in a single click.

- **QRishing (QR Code Phishing) Goes Corporate:** An internal phishing simulation included a QR code on a printed flyer in the breakroom. 30% of employees scanned it with their personal devices...and 8 of them entered work credentials on the spoofed login page. Why did it work? Because no one thought "a hallway flyer" could be an attack vector. (It can)

- **Plugin Panic:** A marketing team installed a third-party browser extension to help with email templates. It quietly exfiltrated inbox data (including customer PII and draft press releases) for *months* before anyone noticed. The extension was "free," because *they* were the product.

- **Auto-Forwarding Fiasco:** An exec's email was compromised. The attacker set up a mail-forwarding rule to an external inbox before IT even knew something was wrong. They spent three weeks thinking the threat actor had been evicted. He was still reading everything. In real time. The cost? The early leak of a confidential acquisition and a 12% drop in stock price.

Final Thought for Chapter 10

The biggest risk in email and web security isn't the attacker.

It's the user who trusts the inbox and the browser like they're sacred.

The attacker doesn't need to find a zero-day.

They just need you to open the door, **click the link,** and **run the malware** for them.

Lock down your inbox. Harden your browsers. Train your people.

Or else they'll party in your network, and you'll be footing the bill.

Quick Wins by Persona

Persona	Quick Win	Why It Matters	Tool/How-To
Individual	Turn on Safe Browsing + use MFA on email	Stops most phishing and web-based drive-bys	Chrome/Firefox settings, Gmail settings
Side-Hustler	Enable SPF/DKIM/DMARC + scan emails	Prevents spoofing, phishing from your domain	Google Workspace, Mailchimp guides, DMARCian
Mid-Cap Boss	Run phishing simulations + restrict macros	Builds awareness + removes a common attack path	KnowBe4, Gophish, M365 Admin Center
Enterprise Exec	Enforce tiered email/web controls + run BEC tabletop	Hardens your top targets + tests what happens when things go wrong	Secure Email Gateway policies, IR tabletop guides

Chapter Eleven

Your Network Isn't Magic—It's Infrastructure (and It's a Mess)

CIS Control 12—Network Infrastructure Management & CIS Control 13—Network Monitoring and Defense

Alternate Title:

"That Firewall You Bought in 2014 Isn't Enough, Champ"

Opening Story: "Everything Looked Fine... Until It Wasn't"

The SOC dashboards were quiet. The firewalls were logging...something. But the network? It was fine...all weekend. When the security team was off duty.

Until it wasn't.

It seems that while the team was enjoying the weekend, attackers had identified an internet-facing server with ***TCP*** port 3389, the default RDP wide open.

In the incident report later, the root cause was easy to trace:

From that exposed remote access port, the moved laterally and established several shells to which they downloaded ransomware. All in about 8 hours.

No segmentation between dev, test, and prod. All internal services became unusable.

And absolutely zero alerts fired when the attacker pivoted into sensitive systems. It wasn't until the ransomware started to deploy that any alerting fired... #Fail

Why? Because the rules were weak, the configurations were outdated, and the logging was noise that no one had tuned...or even checked.

The kicker? The systems were technically *compliant*. They passed the annual checklist. But no one was watching the gaps between those checkboxes.

Because if you build a sloppy network and never look at it again, you might as well hang a "hack me" sign at the border.

This is why **CIS 12 and 13 exist together**. You have to build your network with security in mind AND monitor it like you don't trust it.

Because you shouldn't. Ever.

BLUF (Bottom Line Up Front)

Your network is your castle.

CIS Controls 12 and 13 exist because your network is not surrounded by an enchanted moat.

It's a tangled mess of cables, VLANs, Wi-Fi, SaaS integrations, and old VPN connections no one's reviewed since 2019.

If you're not:

- Locking down your infrastructure configuration
- Disabling risky defaults and legacy protocols
- Monitoring your traffic (and actually looking at, and responding to the alerts)
- Segmenting like your digital life depends on it
- Testing the whole system regularly

...then your network isn't just a risk. It's an invitation.

And attackers RSVP fast.

Let's break it down by persona.

The Individual

"Network security? That's my ISP's job, right?"

Nope. Your router (and everything behind it) is your responsibility. And attackers love home networks because they're usually soft, squishy, and neglected.

What You Should Do:

- **Change default router passwords**. If you haven't done this after reading the past several times it was mentioned, do it now. Seriously. Now. Then go change the defaults on all that smart-crap.

- **Turn off remote admin unless you 100% need it**. And if you don't know what that is, you don't need it.

- **Segment your network**. Put your work devices on one Wi-Fi network, your smart junk (TVs, fridges) on a guest network. Google your specific router for instructions.

- **Disable UPnP and *WPS***. Convenience features are often holes in the wall... and again, if you don't know what these are, one more reason to disable them.

- **Turn on logging...and check it monthly**. If you see IPs from countries you can't spell trying to connect? That's your first clue. See a device you don't recognize, even more fun. If you don't know how to turn on logging (or check it), again...Google your router model.

- **Bonus: Use DNS filtering (like NextDNS or OpenDNS)** to block known bad domains.

Your home network is your personal *DMZ (Demilitarized Zone)*. Lock it down like your bank account depends on it. Because it might.

Quick Win for Individuals:

Task	Why It Matters	Tool/How-To
Kill All Default Passwords	Bad guys love defaults, remove them.	Router admin panel, smart-crap admin panels

The Side-Hustler

"My website is on Shopify. I don't have a network."

You have cloud consoles. APIs. Admin panels. All of which talk to each other...over networks.

And if you run it all from your home network? See above.

What You Need To Lock Down:

- **Restrict admin panels to your IP if possible**. If your platform provides for it, only allow access from specific locations.
- **Enforce MFA everywhere...including on your web host, payment gateway, and domain registrar**.
- **Use Cloudflare or similar to add a WAF to your website. Even the free tier will stop basic attacks**.
- **Check your web server logs weekly for weird access attempts**.
- **Set up alerts on your admin accounts for logins from new locations or devices**. Also monitor your website logs and DNS activity. Anything weird needs to be investigated.

- **Use business-grade routers/firewalls** (not ISP junk).
- **Disable UPnP** and legacy protocols.

Pro Tip: **If you run a dev/test server, NEVER expose it directly to the internet. Use VPN tunnels and/or strong access controls.**

Quick Win for Side-Hustlers:

Task	Why It Matters	Tool/How-To
Enforce MFA everywhere	MFA blocks a huge portion of attacks, and it's easy.	Check all of your accounts, if it has an MFA option, enable it.

The Mid-Cap Boss

"We have a firewall and a VLAN. We're good."

Maybe. But when was the last time anyone:

- Reviewed firewall rules?
- Verified segmentation works (via pen tests or scans)?
- Tuned your ***IDS (Intrusion Detection System)/IPS (Intrusion Prevention System)*** for real-world attacks?
- Audited network diagrams? (Quarterly at a minimum). Update them as part of change control with every cycle (no, seriously).

Additionally, there's some best practices you need to confirm are in place, and if not, put them in place:

- Segment aggressively: Employee, IoT, dev, and guest networks get their own zones.
- Monitor east-west traffic. Not just ingress/egress.
- Block legacy protocols (NetBIOS, SMBv1, Telnet, etc.).
- Alert on new devices appearing in your network.

- Use configuration management tools, and report on drift.

What You Should Be Doing:

- **Network diagrams that are updated and match reality.** Not just the "aspirational" ones from the MSP.
- **Segment based on business function and data sensitivity.** Prod never touches dev. IoT never sees Finance. Period.
- **Use NAC (Network Access Control)** to block rogue devices.
- **Use IDS/IPS tools** (like Snort, Suricata, or commercial options) inside your network, not just at the edge.
- **Monitor east-west traffic, not just north-south.** Attackers pivot internally faster than you think.
- **Tune your firewall and IDS rules quarterly.** Stale rules are security theater.
- **Alert on key behaviors:** large outbound transfers, internal port scans, privilege escalations, lateral movement attempts.

If your SOC dashboard never shows anything interesting? Either you're running a unicorn environment, or your tuning is garbage.

Quick Win for Mid-Cap Bosses:

Task	Why It Matters	Tool/How-To
Document your network(s)	You seriously can't defend what you don't know.	NMap, Intermapper, Device42. If you're in the cloud, use the native cloud mapping tools.

The Enterprise Executive

"We have ZTNA and EDR. Isn't that enough?"

It's a start. But Zero Trust isn't magic. It's also deeper than just Network Access. And if you're not demanding network governance, logging, and internal monitoring tied into your SIEM and risk dashboards...you're just pretending.

What You Should Be Driving:

- **Mandate that network segmentation is validated quarterly via pen tests and red team scenarios.** Not just config reviews. Ideally, ongoing, regular purple team exercises to validate controls (all, not just segmentation) are working. (I know it's "more money", but seriously dude... hope is not a good business strategy.

- **Require logging of all network traffic:** And not just at the firewall, but from applications, cloud, endpoints, and internal switches. Have your security team build you summaries of the logging results (trends, anomalies, blind spots), and review them at the Executive level.

- **Make DNS filtering org-wide** and part of your incident detection stack.

- **Use *NDR (Network Detection and Response)*** to catch what your EDR misses.
- **Insist on real-time alerts** for risky network behaviors tied to business impact.
- **Correlate network events to asset criticality** in your SIEM dashboards.
- **Fund network modernization**. If you're still running flat networks (really?), it's time to get those projects approved.
- **Include supply chain and vendor connections** in your network reviews.

If attackers can pivot across your environment without setting off alarms?
That's not Zero Trust.
That's Zero Visibility.

Quick Win for Enterprise Execs:

Task	Why It Matters	Tool/How-To
Validate visibility	Logging matters, especially when the crap hits the fan. If it's not logged, you have blinders on.	Have your team walk you through your applications and networks, demonstrating where they ***don't*** have logging.

Real-World Fails

- **The "Open VPN" Disaster:** A VPN portal was left open to the internet. Weak creds got brute-forced. Once in? No internal segmentation. They hit everything. Fast.
- **The "Flat Network" Ransomware Party:** Finance, dev, and IoT were all on the same network. A phish got an intern's laptop infected. The ransomware found the whole file server farm in 5 minutes.
- **The "No Logs" Regret:** After a breach, the incident response team couldn't answer the first question from regulators: "How did they get in?" Because the longest any logs were retained was three days.

Final Thought for Chapter 11

Your network isn't static. It's breathing, growing, and if you're not watching, it's leaking.

Building a secure network is like building a castle.

But if no one's watching the walls, the gates, or the sketchy vendor at the back door?

It's not a castle. It's a tourist trap for attackers.

Lock it down.

Watch it constantly.

Don't assume your firewalls, dashboards, and shiny new "Zero Trust" SaaS platform will save you.

They won't if no one's tuning them.

They won't if your network looks the same inside as it does from the parking lot.

And they definitely won't if you never check to see if someone's already inside waving at your file server.

Network hygiene is not set-and-forget.

It's monitor-and-verify.

Forever.

Because attackers don't need an invitation...they just need an overlooked port.

Quick Wins by Persona

Persona	Quick Win	Why It Matters	Tool/How-To
Individual	Change router password + enable WPA3 + Update firmware	Stops drive-by attackers on your Wi-Fi, removes known vulnerabilities	Router admin UI
Side-Hustler	Use business-grade router + disable UPnP, plus the above	Hardens your storefront and apps	Business router/firewall
Mid-Cap Boss	Audit and update network segmentation	Prevents lateral movement and surprises	Network diagrams + scanning tools
Enterprise Exec	Mandate threat hunting on network flows	Validates that detection works (or doesn't)	SIEM, XDR, threat hunting teams

Chapter Twelve

Incidents Happen—and You'd Better Have a Plan

CIS Control 17—Incident Response Management

Alternate Title:

"The Time for Thinking is *Not* After the Malware Hits."

Opening Story: "Wait, What Do We Do Now?"

The alerts were there.

AV flagged a suspicious file on Tuesday.

The EDR detected credential dumping tools on Wednesday.

On Thursday, someone got locked out of an admin account...the ransomware had landed.

Half the company's systems were offline.

The CISO, realizing this was a potential career-ender, shouted across the hastily-organized war room:

"Where's the incident playbook!?"

The security team stared at him blankly.

Sure, there was a *policy*... Buried somewhere in SharePoint, last updated in 2018.

Probably approved by someone who's now selling ***NFT***s... but a playbook?

Meanwhile, backups were encrypted along with the production data.

The Incident Response retainer hadn't been renewed.

The Public Relations (PR) team had no messaging prepared.

And the CEO was already drafting an email to the board—full of wrong assumptions.

The Incident Response Plan was never developed. Because they had a policy. And that ticked the regulatory box.

An Incident Response policy without a fully tested plan with applicable playbooks is security theater of the worst kind.

Lesson:

Your incident response plan can't just exist.

It has to be alive. Ready. And rehearsed.

BLUF (Bottom Line Up Front)

Incidents will happen. Detection and response determine whether it's a minor embarrassment or a business-ending event.

If you're not:

- Detecting real threats (not just log noise)

- Acting fast with defined roles
- Communicating through secure, out-of-band channels
- Practicing your response (including testing those backups)

...then your IR plan is useless paper.

When panic hits, muscle memory saves you.

Let's build it.

The Individual

"If something bad happens... I'll figure it out, right?"

Good luck with that.

You don't rise to the occasion.

You fall to your level of preparation.

And that's the problem. Because now...your bank account was drained, your email was compromised, and your Uber Eats history is suddenly full of late-night kebabs.

But your first clue was when your debit card *stopped working*. Or your friends started getting weird DMs from "you."

That's too late. In previous chapters we talked about auditing login records, connected devices, etc. This is where the rubber hits the road. You need a plan.

What You Should Do:

- **Set up security alerts:**
    - Google, Apple, Microsoft all let you set alerts for suspicious logins, password changes, new device sign-ins. *Turn. Them. On.*
- **Know your recovery paths:**

    - Can you reset your main email account without your phone? Go into security settings and make it so.
    - Do you have access to backup codes for MFA? Those should be in a home safe or lockbox, not a shared Google folder.

- **Practice incident basics:**
    - Lost phone? Wipe it remotely (use Find My iPhone, or Google's Find My Device, or similar)
    - Suspect malware? Disconnect from Wi-Fi and call someone more experienced than you (or start googling on a separate device).

- **Have a "Digital Go Bag":**
    - A password manager, backup MFA codes, a second email, and a contact you can trust when crap hits the fan. Maybe call them once in a while, just to check in.

Remember, the "technical" hack is a possibility. The social-engineering attack is highly probable. Stay heads-up.

Quick Win for Individuals:

Task	Why It Matters	Tool/How-To
Set alerts + define recovery moves	Fast containment of account hijacks	Google/Apple/Security settings, backup plans

The Side-Hustler

"If my Shopify site gets hacked, I'll just... call someone?"

Buddy, no.

Your email got popped, your Shopify account got changed, and your customer list is now being spammed with crypto scams.

By the time you realize you're compromised, you could have customers screaming and payment processors freezing your account.

You don't have an IR team, but you do have an Instagram page and a reputation to lose.

Figure it out now, before it's costing you your business.

Side-Hustler IR 101:

- **Centralize alerts:**
  - Make sure all your services (email, web host, domain registrar, payment systems) are sending alerts to *one secure email inbox,* ideally with MFA. This is a great use-case for Proton or GMX mail. Oh, and turn on a specific sound notification on your phone when something hits that inbox.
- **Backups:**

  - Back up your site, database, and customer data *regularly*. Store those backups off-platform. Not on the same server. And **not** accessible with the same credentials.

- **Incident cheat sheet:**
  - A simple list: (on paper, or at least in a totally separate cloud environment, with different credentials)
    - How to reset your domain registrar
    - Where to revoke API keys
    - How to lock out collaborators or VAs
    - How to recover from your backups (step by step)
- **Plan communication:**
  - Prepare a "something went wrong" customer notification template, because ghosting your buyers when your store is down is how you get roasted *and* sued.

Quick Win for Side-Hustlers:

Task	Why It Matters	Tool/How-To
Centralize alerts + prewrite crisis templates	Rapid containment + communication	Email security settings, crisis comms templates

The Mid-Cap Boss

"We've got an IR plan. I think."

Neat. When was the last time you *tested* it?

Sure, your org has a help desk. Maybe a security person. You run vulnerability scans and email training.

But when someone clicks the wrong thing, and the EDR fires off five high-severity alerts in five minutes, does anyone know who owns what? And what to do?

This is where you get tested, and if you've failed to train, you fail the test.

Mid-Cap IR Moves:

- **Build (and *test*) an Incident Response Plan:**
  - Who declares an incident?
  - Who has authority to shut down systems?
  - Where do you communicate (spoiler: not over email if you're under attack)
  - Who is in the escalation tree, and do we have their phone numbers?
- **Assign clear roles:**

    - IT handles containment
    - Legal handles breach notification
    - Comms handles messaging
    - *Someone* owns the IR plan... you own verifying.

- **Train your team:**
    - Run tabletop exercises quarterly
    - Start simple: "We think we've been phished. What now?"
    - Grow it to: "The entire eComm system is locked, and we're facing a $2 Million ransom. How do we proceed?"

- **Log and correlate:**
    - Everything you can log should be logged until you 100% know it won't be needed under any incident scenario.
    - EDR, firewall, Application logs, Server commands, SaaS logins...if you can't correlate across these, you're missing the full picture.

- **Document and improve:**
    - After every incident (or near miss) and after every table-top exercise, run a postmortem. Update your plan. Don't just forget it happened.

Quick Win for Mid-Cap Bosses:

Task	Why It Matters	Tool/How-To
Tabletop an incident + validate escalation paths	Shortens response time, exposes hidden failures	Internal tabletop planning, IR runbooks

The Enterprise Executive

"We're SOC 2 compliant. We're fine."

Sure. Until your red team (or worse, an auditor) finds an MFA-exempt admin account that nobody knew existed.

Or your SOC triages an alert but waits 72 hours for VP sign-off before disabling access *because the playbook was "under revision."*

Also, you do know that your SOC2, ISO27001, etc... is only as good as the auditor. Right?

Enterprise IR at Scale:

- **Board-level metrics:**
    - ***MTTD (Mean time to detect)***
    - ***MTTR (Mean time to respond)***
    - % of critical alerts triaged within SLA
    - And for the love of Pete, don't allow the "perverse incentive" to creep in... "We're closing ALL THE TICKETS, so we're good!" (Remember Root Cause Analysis?)
- **Authority delegation:**

  - IR escalation shouldn't require a 12-person email chain and an executive séance. Build workflows where action can happen *fast*, not *perfect.*
  - Define all the IR actions, including: Who can declare an incident? Who can shut down production systems? Who owns customer notification decisions?
- **Incident exercises:**
  - Do real drills. On real systems. With execs. In the room.
  - Throw chaos: ransomware on HR's file server, a DDoS during an earnings call, a rogue employee in IT.
- **Invest in correlation:**
  - SIEM, SOAR, XDR: Whatever you're using, it should stitch together multiple signals. If it's just alert fatigue with a nice UI, you're not secure. You're subscribed.
- **Legal readiness:**
  - Know your breach notification windows (GDPR, CCPA, SEC 10-K, etc.) Have comms prepared and ready to send...just fill in the necessary details.
  - Keep a template press release, lawyer contact list, and cyber insurance and forensics team hotline on file. If you're self-insured, at least have a Breach Response service on speed-dial.

Quick Win for Enterprise Execs:

Task	Why It Matters	Tool/How-To
Conduct live-fire IR + legal/PR prep	Prevents deer-in-headlights response under pressure	IR runbooks, cyber insurance breach coaches, outside counsel

Real-World Fails

- **The "VPN Misconfiguration" Ransomware:** A misconfigured VPN allowed attackers into an enterprise network. The SIEM flagged anomalous lateral movement for two days, but the alerts were buried under noise. By the time someone noticed, domain controllers were already encrypted. Ransom notes followed immediately after.
- **The "Deleted Alert Email" Breach:** A mid-sized financial org received multiple high-severity alerts from their EDR. The email was filtered to a folder marked "Low Priority" by a well-meaning intern. Nobody opened it for two weeks. The attackers had a field day during that time. Massive data breach, with legal, regulatory, and reputational damage to spare.
- **The "We've Never Tested This" IR Disaster:** A healthcare provider had a 32-page incident response plan. It had never been rehearsed. When ransomware hit, no one knew how to contact legal, the comms team posted on Twitter *before* containment, and the backups hadn't been tested since 2019... and they didn't work.
- **The "We Let the Vendor Handle It" Confusion:** A SaaS

> vendor was breached, and customer data was likely exposed. The client company had no monitoring in place to detect exfiltration or credential reuse. Worse, they had no contract clause requiring breach notifications. So they found out via Reddit.

If it's your customer's data, it's your reputation...no matter who you outsource to.

Final Thought for Chapter 12

If you only detect...you're slow.

If you only respond...you're sloppy.

If you **detect, escalate, contain, recover, and communicate...you survive.**

Train like you fight. Fight like you trained. No excuses.

Quick Wins by Persona

Persona	Quick Win	Why It Matters	Tool/How-To
Individual	Enable login notifications + backup recovery options	Early detection of hijacked accounts	Google/Apple/Security settings, Authenticator backups
Side-Hustler	Build a one-pager IR cheat sheet	Speed and clarity during small-biz chaos	List account resets, contacts, and key backups
Mid-Cap Boss	Conduct your first tabletop	Exposes gaps in response roles and processes	Use a simple phishing scenario and a timer
Enterprise Exec	Review MTTD/MTTR quarterly + test real-world escalation	Aligns leadership expectations with operational reality	IR metrics dashboard + exec-involved simulation

Chapter Thirteen

Policies Without Power

CIS Control 14—Security Awareness and Skills Training & CIS Control 4—Secure Configuration of Enterprise Assets and Software

Alternate Title:

"The Stuff No One Reads... Until the FBI is Involved."

Opening Story: "We Had Policies. No One Read Them."

Ransomware sucks rocks. It's brutal, and sometimes final, because even if you pay the ransom, about 20% still never get their data back. For those that do, it often takes weeks to decrypt all the files, and longer to get systems back to full functionality.

A CISO talking to the VP of IT after a ransomware incident had taken out half the org's operations stated:

"We have a policy against standing up any test box with a publicly-exposed port, and also against leaving any sandbox system running beyond 72 hours. This shouldn't have happened!"

The VP fired back:

"You never shared it with us."

"It was in the policy repo with every other policy," the CISO retorted.

"Nobody can find anything in there, and you know it!" came the exasperated response.

The real-world implementation?

- Zero enforcement.
- No metrics.
- No buy-in.
- Just words.
- Lots of them.
- Not a single one printed on an incident response checklist.

Governance isn't about paperwork...it's about power.

It's how you prioritize, measure, fund, and enforce your security program.

Without it, you're flying blind with a binder full of rules tucked under a desk somewhere and no way to see if they're working.

BLUF (Bottom Line Up Front)

Governance is how you make security real.

CIS Control 14 and CIS Control 4 exist because policies, metrics, and leadership alignment are what elevate security from "that thing IT does" to "an integrated business function."

If you're not:

- Writing policies people can easily find, easily read, and easily understand
- Mapping controls to real risks
- Measuring effectiveness (not just activity)
- Driving executive ownership and cross-functional accountability
- Building governance into budgets, boards, and decision cycles

...then your "governance program" is sock-puppet theater.

And as you've seen across this book, security theater ends in real breaches.

Let's break it down by persona, because yes, even your side-hustle needs a policy or two.

The Individual

"Governance? What am I supposed to govern—my Netflix history?"

Fair point.

But governance at the individual level means defining your own rules for how you manage your digital life.

If you don't build habits, you'll default to chaos, and chaos is vulnerable.

What You Should Do:

- **Make yourself a policy:** A short doc or checklist that covers your update cadence, backup routine, and password hygiene.

- **Define your tech boundaries:** Are you willing to visit sketchy sites? What devices can access your sensitive accounts? Where do you store backups? Define these and more. Then stick to them.

- **Review quarterly:** Add reminders to your calendar. Audit yourself.

- **Write a digital contingency plan:** If something happens to you, can your family access your accounts? Do you have recovery documented?

Governance for individuals isn't about control…it's about clarity. You don't have a CISO. You *are* the CISO.

Quick Win for Individuals:

Task	Why It Matters	Tool/How-To
Create personal tech policies + update quarterly	Prevents digital chaos, protects identity	Simple checklists, recurring reminders

The Side-Hustler

"I have a spreadsheet. That's governance, right?"

Nice start.

But governance isn't just tracking things, it's defining expectations, building accountability, and planning for when (not if) something goes wrong.

It's thinking through the various challenges you might encounter, and building plans to deal with each. Then practicing, testing, and ensuring they work.

That empire you're building from your kitchen table can only survive the attacks you've prepared it to survive...so prepare well.

Side-Hustle Governance Basics:

- **Create a one-page security policy:** Passwords, data handling, third-party tool use, and financial transactions.
- **Define breach response steps:** What happens if you get hacked? Write your customer notification template *now*, not after.
- **Set measurable goals:** MFA, backups, phishing training. Track monthly.

- **Understand your legal exposure:** Payment data? Email lists? GDPR and CCPA apply even to side hustles.

Quick Win for Side-Hustlers:

Task	Why It Matters	Tool/How-To
Build mini governance docs + crisis templates	Turns chaos into recoverable events	1-page policies, incident playbooks

The Mid-Cap Boss

"We have policies and a risk register."

Awesome.

But are they driving behavior? Or just sitting on SharePoint?

Ask yourself these questions:

- **Do your people actually know where they are?**
- **Have they read them?**
- **Do they follow them?**
- **Believe in them?**
- **And most importantly, do they see you following them?**

People need to be trained on how to use policies. And policies need to have procedural documents to support them. So your people both know what to do, and how to do it.

And you need to lead. Quote policy often. Adhere to the policies. Hold people accountable to the policies so they know you are both aware of, and will enforce them. Create a culture of policy adherence, and those policies will actually do something more than collect dust.

What Real Governance Looks Like:

- **Update policies regularly:** At least annually. Track revisions.
- **Link policies to metrics:** If you say "lock inactive accounts in 30 days," measure it.
- **Assign ownership:** Every policy has a name attached. Every control has a reviewer.
- **Drive cross-functional buy-in:** HR, Legal, Finance, IT...everyone plays.
- **Push governance reporting up:** Board decks. Executive scorecards. Budget planning cycles.

Quick Wins for Mid-Cap Bosses

Task	Why It Matters	Tool/How-To
Tie policies to live metrics + review quarterly	Shows effectiveness, not just existence	*GRC* platforms, KPI tracking

The Enterprise Executive

"We have a GRC platform and quarterly board reporting. We're very mature."

Maybe, Viktor.

But real governance **changes behavior**...it doesn't just create prettier spreadsheets. Just like the points covered in the Mid-Cap Boss section, culture is king. Do all the things mentioned there, and then elevate it,

Ask yourself some questions:

- Are my policies applicable to my business? (Did you just download a package-deal from some legal firm for $500 and call it good?)

- Are my Policies easily understood? (Plain language and actionable statements are key... your readers aren't lawyers.}

- How do I measure compliance? (This is how you can tell if the first two bullets had wrong answers)

What You Should Be Driving:

- **Tie security to business outcomes**: Instead of reporting "phishing simulation results," show "reduction in real-world phish click-throughs that could have triggered financial loss." Risk reduction, not just click reduction.

- **Fund security like a business function**: Define your risk appetite (the amount of dollars you're willing to lose to a cyber attack), and have your security leadership build a protection plan to that level. That becomes your Protection Level Agreement (PLA). If the dollars needed from security to meet your PLA exceed the amount you're willing to lose, you need to re-align.

- **Push policy relevance**: Require policies to be written in plain language. Score them for clarity, accessibility, and implementation. When a breach happens, and the regulators review your policies, they'll ask about your adherence to them, not their existence.

- **Drive governance by design**: Bake security reviews into all major changes: Product launches, M&A events, cloud migrations, vendor onboarding. If you're tracking DLP events, map them to potential legal exposure, not just volume. And give all of this time and resources, not just lip service.

- **Measure program effectiveness:**
    - % of controls tied to measurable outcomes
    - % of metrics mapped to monetary risk
    - % of incidents traced back to governance failures

Quick Win for Enterprise Execs:

Task	Why It Matters	Tool/How-To
Embed governance into ops, finance, legal, and product cycles	Creates security by design, not accident	GRC + cross-functional planning

Real World Fails

- **The "It Was in the Policy" Incident (a.k.a. the opener):** The CISO had written the rule: No test systems should expose public ports or live past 72 hours. But the policy was buried, unread, and unenforced. The test box got popped. The system got ransomed. Turns out, "we had a policy" doesn't help if no one knew it existed.

- **The "Audit File Dust Bunny" Disaster:** A healthcare org proudly passed their ISO 27001 audit. Six months later, they were breached via a vendor integration with no MFA. The governance doc *technically* required MFA, but the policy was outdated and never enforced. The auditor had reviewed the docs, not the implementation. The patients? Not impressed.

- **The "Third Party, Third Rail" Problem:** A SaaS company onboarded a vendor who provided "data enrichment" services. No vendor review. No DPA. No security questionnaire. That vendor got breached and exposed sensitive PII. When the CEO asked, "How did this happen?" the governance controller said, "We didn't know they had that data." The vendor *did*. Governance *didn't*.

- **The "No One Owns It" Melt-Down:** A major financial firm had 50+ security policies... and zero named owners. During an investigation, legal needed to know who was responsible for enforcing vendor risk assessments. The answer? Shrug emoji. They had five different "vendor" policies... all out of date. Governance without accountability = governance theater.

Final Thought for Chapter 13

Governance isn't about being able to say,

"We had a policy."

It's about being able to prove:

"We *followed* the policy. We *measured* it. And it *worked*."

Otherwise, your "security policies" are just letters in a file.

And attackers don't care how well you formatted your PDF.

Quick Wins by Persona

Persona	Quick Win	Why It Matters	Tool/How-To
Individual	Create and maintain your digital contingency plan	If you're incapacitated, or your identity gets owned, you'll need it.	Create an analog binder (with written and printed docs) with all of your recovery codes for all accounts.
Side-Hustler	Document and follow your improvement plan (with milestones)	Tracking, and documenting your successes (MFA, Backups, IR Plan, etc) gives you confidence	Set the milestones in your calendar, document them in a spreadsheet, go out for Sushi when you achieve a milestone.
Mid-Cap Boss	Create measurable metrics tied to business risk.	You'll gain credibility with leadership, and you'll show progress as it happens.	Use FAIR (Factor Analysis of Information Risk) or another risk modeling approach.
Enterprise Exec	Drive "Governance by Design"	Moves the governance conversation to the far left and ensures higher compliance.	Start asking for design review summaries for key projects, showing how governance is incorporated.

Chapter Fourteen

The Outsiders

CIS Controls 15—Service Provider Management & CIS Control 16—Application Software Security

Alternate Title:

"The Call Is Coming From Outside the Firewall."

Opening Story: "We Trusted Them. They Let Us Down."

A fast-growing retailer spun up an e-commerce site using a third-party marketing agency. The agency used a freelance developer to build a custom checkout plugin.

That plugin was perfect...easy, fast, clean.

It was also riddled with vulnerabilities.

- No input sanitization.
- Payment token data exposure.
- A default admin backdoor left "for maintenance access."

The developer left the agency six months later.

Two months after that, attackers found the backdoor.

Two weeks after that, customer credit cards started getting skimmed.

No one noticed, because no one monitored the plugin.

No contract required code security reviews.

No vendor governance existed beyond "Did they deliver on time?"

The breach cost millions.

The brand took a major hit.

And worst of all?

The retailer didn't even write the code that got them owned!

BLUF (Bottom Line Up Front)

If you're using someone else's software, infrastructure, or service...

you've extended your attack surface to include **their** mistakes.

- CIS Control 15 exists because service providers are part of your security now, whether you like it or not.

- CIS Control 16 exists because modern apps are stitched together with open-source, third-party, and vendor-supplied code...and *all* of it can go bad.

If you're not:

- Vetting vendors for security hygiene

- Reviewing their breach history prior to engagement

- Requiring contracts with teeth
- Reviewing their access rights regularly
- Testing software for vulnerabilities before production
- Monitoring code dependencies after release

...you're not outsourcing risk.

You're **importing it**.

In bulk.

With express shipping.

The Individual

"It's just an app from the Play Store..."

Maybe.

But Play Store ≠ Safe Store.

Just ask the millions who downloaded flashlight apps that secretly mined crypto or logged keystrokes.

What You Should Do:

- **Install apps only from trusted sources:** Google Play, Apple App Store. No shady APKs from Reddit. No cracked apps. Ever.
- **Check app permissions:** Your calculator app does not need microphone, location, and camera access.
- **Audit browser extensions:** Delete junk monthly. Only install official releases.
- **Watch for takeover signs:** If an app updates and gets *weird* (ads, pop-ups, battery drain) nuke it from orbit.
- **Be cautious with free software:** If you're not paying, you're the product...or worse, the stepping stone.

Quick Win for Individuals:

Task	Why It Matters	Tool/How-To
Regularly audit installed apps/extensions	Cuts exposure from takeover, backdoors	Phone settings, browser extension managers

The Side-Hustler

"I just use a few plugins and APIs..."

And each of them could be your weakest link.

What You Should Lock Down:

- **Vet plugins and integrations:** Update history? Verified developer? Code repo available?
- **Use official integrations:** Stripe, Zapier, Google APIs...stick to the blessed paths.
- **Track contractor code:** Freelancers? Ask if they wrote it themselves, checked dependencies, scanned for vulnerabilities.
- **Limit API scopes:** Never grant "admin" when "read-only" suffices.
- **Back up everything:** Lock-in and breach risks don't announce themselves first.

Quick Win for Side-Hustlers:

Task	Why It Matters	Tool/How-To
Inventory and permission-check plugins and apps	Prevents external compromise via suppliers	WordPress security plugins, manual audits

The Mid-Cap Boss

"We have vendors and apps. We trust them."

Do you though?

Trust is the easy path. It's just like hope. No effort. But it's fraught with danger and nearly always ends badly.

"Trust but verify" is the better option, and not just in international relations. You're in a contractual relationship with a vendor. Did you bake security into that contract? And if you did, how are you validating that the contract is being fulfilled? Hard questions. And they require effort to answer.

Nobody said business was going to be easy. And you were hired to make the business successful. So get to work and start verifying the trust you place in your vendors and suppliers. You'll likely be surprised by what you find *isn't* happening.

And this doesn't just apply to your vendors and suppliers. Internal trust also needs to be verified. Ten admins with root privileges on your core AWS account is a nightmare waiting to happen... you may trust all ten, but if one gets popped, that trusted identity is now rogue, and is going to put you out of business.

Controls You Should Already Have:

- **Vendor risk assessments:** Before onboarding any new vendor. Not just questionnaires...real assessment. Use paid services (BitSight, OneTrust, Upguard), or at a minimum do interviews.
- **Contracts with teeth:** Include breach notifications, audit rights, and security SLAs with monetary penalties.
- **Access reviews:** What systems do vendors touch? When was it last reviewed? What are the security controls in place?
- **Secure *SDLC (Software Development LifeCycle)*:**
    - Dependency scanning (Snyk, Dependabot)
    - Threat modeling (with documentation)
    - SAST/DAST before go-live
- **Third-party library tracking:** Especially for critical apps. Correlate CVEs with library resources.

Quick Win for Mid-Cap Bosses:

Task	Why It Matters	Tool/How-To
Tie vendors to risk tiers + require evidence	Shrinks inherited risk footprint	Contract templates, vendor portals, SIG-Lite assessments

The Enterprise Executive

"Our vendors are ISO-certified and our apps are built in-house."

Cool.

Now prove that matters. Just because they carry a certification doesn't mean they're secure. Just because your own employees built an app, doesn't mean they did it securely. Validation is king. Without it, you're the serf. And the Visigoths are coming.

What You Should Be Driving:

- **Vendor Tiering:** Rank by criticality + data access + risk. More critical = more scrutiny.

- **Security scorecards:** Monitor vendor security postures (SecurityScorecard, BitSight).

- **SBOMs:** Software Bill of Materials for all critical apps.

- **Open-source governance:** Track dependencies. Monitor vulnerabilities. Update proactively.

- **Supply chain tabletop exercises:** Simulate third-party compromise scenarios.

Quick Win for Enterprise Execs:

Task	Why It Matters	Tool/How-To
Integrate vendors into risk and resilience frameworks	Extends your control boundary	RiskRegister, GRC platforms, IR tabletop exercises

Real-World Fails

- A marketing automation vendor got phished, and attackers pivoted through the platform to send malware-laced emails *from* their customer's domains.
- A SaaS CRM leaked thousands of client notes due to a bad config in a third-party hosting partner.
- A legal firm embedded a malicious PDF ***SDK*** into case files because their developer downloaded a "free" PDF editor library without scanning it first.

Final Thought for Chapter 14

The old perimeter model said:

"Keep the bad guys outside."

Today's model says:

"Half your environment *is* outside. Good luck."

If you don't verify, monitor, and manage third parties like they're already inside your walls—you're not securing your business.

You're just outsourcing the breach notification.

Quick Wins by Persona

Persona	Quick Win	Why It Matters	Tool/How-To
Individual	Become your own auditor	When you take the time to look, you find… and can fix.	Create a spreadsheet of all your devices and apps. List the permissions each has, if the defaults have been changes, etc. Revist quarterly over pizza.
Side-Hustler	Write "Least Privilege" on your mirror, then start restricting permissions	Over-privileged resources (apps, devices, etc.) are regularly leveraged by baddies.	If you are cloud-based, use native config managers, app scanners, and access managers. If not, do it manually and document your findings.
Mid-Cap Boss	Build a robust Secure Software Development Lifecycle	Your software is your soft-spot, and it faces the world.	Snyk, dependebot, Hurosec. Software Composition Analysis tools, SAST, etc.
Enterprise Exec	Build in Third-party compromises into your table tops	You'll find out just how vulnerable some of your vendors can make you.	Start with your top three vendors, enumerate all of their connections into your systems, and threat-model each. Then start in on the rest.

Chapter Fifteen

People, Clicks, and Other Unpatched Vulnerabilities

CIS Control 14—Security Awareness and Skills Training

Alternate Title:

"Your Staff Isn't Stupid. Your Training Is."

Opening Story, Part 1: "Hi, I'm Your New Security Guy. Also... You've Been Hacked."

It was my first day on the job as head of cybersecurity.

I hadn't even figured out how to connect to the printer when I got the call...from the CFO, no less.

He was panicked.

"We just sent $100,000 to a vendor, but...they didn't receive it. I think we got scammed."

He wasn't wrong.

A quick forensic pass told the story.

Someone had compromised our controller's email account and set up a forwarding rule...silently piping copies of every message to an external address.

That morning, a reply showed up in a real email thread.

It included the entire conversation history, looked completely legit, and came from a domain that was visually identical to the vendor's, except for one swapped character from the Cyrillic alphabet. Classic lookalike domain.

The attacker waited for just the right moment, injected the fraudulent message, and told the controller to send the funds to a "new account."

Which he did.

Fortunately, the CFO was sharp. He was already on the phone with the bank.

While he worked the financial angle, I had IT kill all forwarding rules in Outlook Web Access and force password resets for every user with forwarding configured.

By some miracle (or maybe just timing) we got lucky. The funds hadn't settled yet. The bank clawed them back.

Had it taken another hour, that money would've been gone.

Moving forward, I instructed the Finance Team to track all attempts at ***BEC (Business Email Compromise)***, and submit the data to the ***FBI's IC3 (Internet Crime Complaint Center)*** site (www.ic3.gov). Although enforcement and prosecution is pretty rare, at least they'd be contributing to the database of these attempts.

Opening Story, Part 2: "Training Isn't a Waste—Here's the Proof."

Years later, I got a call from the FBI.

(And no, not because I was in trouble.)

They were reaching out because over the years our finance team had submitted reports of BEC attempts through the IC3 (Internet Crime Complaint Center), just like they'd been trained to.

They'd spotted spoofed vendor emails. Captured the headers. Forwarded it, flagged it, and submitted it...no hesitation, no confusion.

Turns out, we weren't the only org doing that.

But we were one of the few doing it **consistently**.

And it made a difference.

The FBI had identified, arrested, and was prosecuting the actor behind a coordinated BEC ring.

They needed a statement from me to support the case.

That's when it hit me: **training works**.

Awareness works.

People can become your strongest line of defense.

But not by accident.

Not with boring slide decks.

Not if you treat security like a once-a-year compliance exercise.

BLUF (Bottom Line Up Front)

Security awareness isn't a checkbox, it's the control that determines whether a phishing email becomes a breach, or a win for your IR plan.

CIS Control 14 exists because most incidents start with a human:

- Clicking something they shouldn't

- Ignoring something they shouldn't
- Trusting something that never deserved it

You are already a target.
Your users are already targets.
The only question is whether you've trained them well enough to spot the trap, report the bait, and shut it down.

Let's see how this plays out by persona.

The Individual

"I'm not worth targeting."

You absolutely are. Especially to support scam call centers, ransomware-as-a-service outfits, and opportunistic info-stealers. I've seen tens of thousands of dollars in cash walk out the door (literally) into the hands of bad guys just on one successful targeting.

Most attacks start not with "you've been hacked" but "your system is at risk." Neon-red pop-ups. Loud beeping. Fake Microsoft reps with perfect phone manners and remote access tools that promise to help... and instead empty your savings account.

What You Should Do:

- **Recognize the scam pattern:**
    - "Your computer is infected."
    - "Call Microsoft Support now."
    - "Install this utility so we can fix it." (NEVER do this)

All of these are bogus, and you need to mentally prepare to ignore them. Microsoft isn't reaching out to you to tell you that your computer is infected. Ever. In fact, any unsolicited contact by anyone that suggests you have a problem they can solve is total BS… or at a minimum a sales attempt for something you absolutely don't need.

- **Don't visit, click-through, or download fixes on sketchy sites.** No registry cleaner, battery optimizer, or "Java update" is worth getting keylogged.

- **If your screen locks up and starts yelling at you:**

    - Disconnect from Wi-Fi.

    - Force a shutdown (hold power).

    - Call someone you trust…NOT the number on the screen (if you don't have that person, Google the solution from a different device. Most of the time, clearing your browser cache solves the issue).

- **Talk about scams with family.** Especially seniors. These scumbag criminals target those least able to resist their aggressive approaches, and least able to recover financially.

- **Follow some credible security pros on socia**l (Twitter/X, LinkedIn). Find the ones who explain things like a human, not like they're casting a Linux spell (we cyber-types are soooo guilty of tech-talk)

- **Take a 15-minute phishing test** once a month: GoPhish, SpeedPhish, Phishing Box, Jigsaw, etc.

- **Read headlines** from TheHackerNews, and check HaveIBeenPwned.com…if your email is listed, change passwords

- **Get familiar with spotting sketchy links** (hover over the link and view, don't click)

You might be the only "security guy" in your house, but there are resources everywhere... **use them**.

Quick Win for Individuals:

Task	Why It Matters	Tool/How-To
Practice scam spotting and incident reporting	Builds instinct to pause and verify	IC3.gov reporting, FBI scam alerts

The Side-Hustler

"I've got too much on my plate to do training."

Sure. Until your Gmail gets phished and someone redirects your Shopify payout.

Because if you take card payments, you're a potential Magecart host... and your client list likely includes payment info (because you've not yet learned about PCI compliance requirements).

Because your inbox is full of invoices, Stripe tokens, and credentials.

And because attackers don't need to know your revenue to launch a convincing phish, which launches ransomware...and ruins your day.

Remember the opening story? That wasn't a CISO at a Fortune 500. That was someone dealing with a vendor wire transfer...and one well-crafted email almost cost six figures.

Awareness You Actually Need

- Learn to recognize vendor impersonation emails ("Stripe needs verification..."). Everything should be scrutinized.
- Train your VA or contractors...make it part of onboarding. Use free training from Microsoft, NIST, ***CIRT***, etc.
- Use phishing simulations on yourself (as described in the

Individual section above). It's like playing whack-a-mole with your own bad habits.

- Sign up for alerting services that warn of new scam patterns (e.g., from your registrar, Google Alerts, CIRT, FBI IC3, etc.). If you're waiting to learn about scams from Reddit or your mom's Facebook group, you're already behind.

You're a company now. Start acting like one...especially when it comes to educating the humans with access to your systems.

What You Should Lock Down:

- **Train yourself and your contractors:**
  If they touch your tools, they need to spot phishing, spoofing, and scams. They also need to understand OWASP and other security frameworks.

- **Enable email forwarding detection:**
  If Gmail/Outlook forwards everything to an unfamiliar domain, you're compromised. Turn on notification to your notification email address (that separate one we discussed in Chapter 12, under *Centralized Alerts*) anytime forwarding is enabled.

- **Plan breach response:**
  Have a template ready for notifying customers if needed. Maybe even one for each of a few scenarios. Better over-prepared than not at all.

- **Bookmark IC3.gov:**
  Submit BEC attempts and fraud attempts immediately.

Quick Win for Side-Hustlers:

Task	Why It Matters	Tool/How-To
Train VAs/contractors + monitor account behaviors	Stops insider threats and external phish	Gmail/Outlook rules, phishing awareness

The Mid-Cap Boss

"We mandate security training annually."

OK...so is it:

- Annual?
- Boring?
- Ignored?
- Rolled out to everyone identically?

Not Cool. Then it's **compliance...not culture.**

The worst training is the kind people sleep through. The best training builds confidence, pattern recognition, and a culture of reporting without shame. Find engaging ways to train... and stop mailing it in.

How to Make Awareness Not Suck

- **Segment training:** Sales doesn't need the same depth as Engineering, but Finance needs to know about BEC scams. Targeted training makes your team less targetable.
- **Gamify it:** Add competitions, leaderboards, or rewards for high performance (random drawing of gift cards for those who passed

the phishing test, maybe even an annual Nintendo give-away)

- **Supplement with phishing simulations**: Gophish, Microsoft Attack Simulator, KnowBe4

- **Capture metrics:** Who clicked, who reported, who ignored. Then tailor support, not punishment

- **Normalize curiosity:** Build a Slack channel for "Is this phish?"...you'll be shocked how much people engage

Training is a control. Make it measurable. Make it memorable. Make it matter.

How to Make Awareness Stick:

- **Segment training:**
  Sales, finance, HR, and engineering face different threats. Train accordingly.

- **Gamify it:**
  Leaderboards, raffles, positive reinforcement for phish catches.

- **Simulate constantly:**
  Phishing tests, ***social engineering*** calls, QR code bait. Real-world tactics.

- **Debrief failures:**
  Use real incidents (anonymized) to show how gaps create breaches.

- **Measure what matters:**
  Not just "click rate," but "reporting rate" and "escalation speed."

Quick Win for Mid-Cap Bosses:

Task	Why It Matters	Tool/How-To
Move from checkbox training to behavior-driven reinforcement	Culture eats compliance for breakfast	Gophish, KnowBe4, Slack/Teams "Is this phish?" channels

The Enterprise Executive

"We have low click rates in phishing simulations."

Metrics can be gamed.

Culture can't. So... a few questions:

- Are the metrics real, or gamed? (i.e., are your managers rewarded for presenting good numbers, or real numbers?)

- Do the people exempt from training...have the most privileged access? Looking at you, CEO, i.e. if your email gets popped, it's not just phishing, it's front-page news.

- Do you include social engineering in red team/penetration tests (pen test for short)?

- **Do your vendors train their staff?**
  Third parties are often the weakest human link. Require proof of awareness programs in vendor onboarding.

- When's the last time your *board* took a phishing test? Or any training? Or had a vulnerability assessment conducted on them? It can be eye-opening on several levels.

What You Should Be Driving:

- **Tie training to exec KPIs:**
  If leaders don't care, users won't either. Build KPIs on both phishing training, as well as domain-specific training for developers, systems teams, etc.

- **Force exec participation:**
  No exemptions. No exceptions. And highlight their participation (maybe even a little of the fails to prove we're all human)

- **Use threat modeling:**
  Train based on your actual attack patterns, not generic phish.

- **Map training to IR:**
  When someone clicks, they need to know exactly how to escalate. Especially if that click is on a critical system... the SOC needs to be engaged now.

- **Enforce vendor training:**
  Third parties with access = mandatory awareness programs.

That last bullet is important. Don't forget your third parties.
Vendors with access to your network should have to show proof of security awareness programs too. And not just a "yes, we have a program" on the questionnaire.
Your people might not click, but your partner's receptionist might.

Quick Win for Enterprise Execs:

Task	Why It Matters	Tool/How-To
Align awareness with threat models + incident response	Embeds detection instincts across org	Phish-runbooks, training refreshers, exec participation

Real-World Fails

- **The "Annual Training" Breach:** An employee at a healthcare company completed their required security awareness training... 11 months ago. They clicked a phishing link, entered their credentials, and unknowingly granted access to protected health information. The breach affected over 45,000 patient records. The root cause? Human error? The remediation? A strongly worded email... and the same training module next year... so, really, root cause was culture error.

- **The "CEO Exempt" Compromise:** An executive exempt from security training and phishing simulations was targeted by a well-crafted vendor spoof email. They approved a wire transfer for $750,000...sent to an attacker-controlled account. When asked why they didn't verify the request, they said, "It looked legit." When asked why they were exempt from training, no one had an answer.

- **The "Red Team Got In With a Clipboard" Test:** A red team engagement tested both technical and human defenses. Technical defenses held. The humans? Not so much. An actor with a fake badge, a clipboard, and a confident walk was granted access to a secure floor, a network jack, and coffee. They were able to drop a device, gain internal access, and simulate data exfiltration...all without triggering a single technical alert. This story plays out ALL THE TIME in red-team engagements.

- **The "Nobody Asked the Vendor" Fallout:** A third-party marketing firm was given access to a company's web analytics platform. The firm's junior analyst clicked a phishing email and reused their company password. The attacker didn't just access analytics...they used the session to pivot into the customer database via a linked CRM. The vendor had no security awareness training, and the contract had no requirements for one. Oops.

Final Thought for Chapter 15

Security awareness isn't about *compliance.* It's about *culture.*

You can buy all the tech in the world. You can deploy MFA, roll out EDR, segment your networks, and hire a red team with their own merch.

But none of that matters if your people still click the phishing link.

Humans aren't the weakest link...they're just the least supported.

Give them real training, not checkbox training.

Give them room to ask dumb questions...before they make expensive mistakes.

Give them tools, habits, and a reason to care.

Because the difference between a phishing click and a phishing report might just be one Slack message that says: **"Hey, is this weird?"**

Reward that message. Build *that* culture.

Or you'll spend a whole lot more rewarding a ransomware actor instead.

Quick Wins by Persona

Persona	Quick Win	Why It Matters	Tool/How-To
Individual	Follow 2–3 security pros + take monthly phishing tests	Keeps threat awareness fresh and builds real-world intuition	Twitter/X, Jigsaw Phishing Quiz, HackerNews
Side-Hustler	Train VAs and use phishing tests on yourself	Reduces human error exposure in tiny teams with big risk	Free training + alert services (CISA, Google)
Mid-Cap Boss	Segment and gamify training + run phishing sims	Drives engagement and reduces click rates across departments	Gophish, KnowBe4, leaderboard with prizes
Enterprise Exec	Include leadership in training + real-world testing	Avoids "VIP immunity" while validating culture and controls	Tailored phishing sims + tabletop IR drills

Chapter Sixteen

Punch Yourself in the Face

CIS Control 18—Penetration Testing

Alternate Title:

"Testing Isn't Paranoia, It's Proof"

Opening Story: "We Hacked Ourselves... And Got Yelled At"

It was a joint red-team/blue-team cyber exercise, scheduled to run alongside a major multi-service military event. The target? A real-world North American defense weapon system, the kind that doesn't just protect a base, but a whole continent.

We were on blue team, defending. The red team was run by a partner organization; exceptionally skilled, creative, persistent. The weapon system operators had been told there would be cyber activity during the exercise, but they probably assumed it would be a few nuisance pings off to the side. Not a full-blown offensive op.

They were wrong.

By the time we identified malicious activity, the red team was deep in the ***kill chain***. Before we even started containment, they'd reached the core interface for the weapon system, and splashed every operator's screen with a laughing skull and crossbones, overlaid with the taunting phrase:

"We are owned you. You can do nothing."

Classic ***ESL*** hacker language. And brutal.

Fortunately, they were wrong too.

Our systems were built with resiliency in mind. Logs were detailed. Backups were recent. And thanks to fast coordination between teams, we restored functionality quickly. But the real wake-up call came afterward.

The two-star general responsible for that weapon system? He was *lit*. I found myself in his office with my commanding officer, fielding direct questions from a very serious man with a very large responsibility. He wanted to know exactly how this could happen, and why his operations had been left so vulnerable.

We laid it out clearly: cyber defense doesn't stop at the firewall. If your systems are running software that's a decade out of date, patching once every three years (or never), and no one's actively probing it like an adversary would... then your risk is measured in months, not years. And recovery isn't guaranteed.

To his credit, that general didn't just get mad, he got moving. Within weeks, the processes for updating and hardening program-managed weapon systems started a serious overhaul.

Because after that day, no one wanted to see that skull again.

BLUF (Bottom Line Up Front)

If you've never tested your defenses, you don't actually know how they'll hold up.

CIS Control 18 exists because hoping your security works is not the same as knowing it works.

This control is about attacking yourself, on purpose, before someone else does.

And no, it's not just for billion-dollar organizations.

There's a version for everyone.

The Individual

"Pen test? I don't even know what a firewall is."

Fair statement, and not surprising.

But you do have a digital life worth testing.

You're your own red team, whether you know it or not. And it's worth getting good at it.

What You Should Do:

- **Audit yourself:** Log into your router (call back to previous chapters). Check what ports are open. See what devices are connected. If anything surprises you, congratulations, you just found a vulnerability. Then, try logging into your router from a new device...check your router logs and see if that shows up (hint: it should)

- **Check your credentials:** Use tools like HaveIBeenPwned.com or Mozilla Monitor. If your email is in a breach, treat that like a red-team finding and make changes accordingly (refer to all the previous chapters).

- **Try your backups:** Can you recover your files from iCloud or Google Drive if your device is lost? Can you log in without your phone?

- **Google yourself:** What does an attacker see when they search your name? That's your initial attack surface.

- **Test your paranoia:** Try spoofing your own phone number *(legal gray area, so research first)*, and use the phishing tests mentioned in chapter 12, occasionally send yourself a fake phishing link. Would you click it?

You're not too small to be attacked. So learn what it feels like to find a gap, before someone else does it for you.

Quick Win for Individuals:

Task	Why It Matters	Tool/How-To
Audit router/devices/online footprint quarterly	Reduce attack surface	Router UI, HaveIBeenPwned, Google search

The Side-Hustler

"My site isn't worth hacking."

Attackers disagree.

If you collect payments, use emails, or run a public site, you are 100% on someone's hit list... because your IP is visible, and they've been probing it.

If they can steal your data, redirect your users to their own site, or ransom you, they ultimately will.

How to Run a Mini-Red Team:

- **Scan your website:** Use Mozilla Observatory, OWASP ZAP, Sucuri SiteCheck, or WPScan if on WordPress.

- **Try basic recon:** Run *whois* on your domain. What info is exposed? Look up subdomains. Search your domain on Shodan.io.

- **Hire a hacker:** Platforms like HackerOne or Bugcrowd offer affordable bug bounty options (with vetted researchers). Even a scoped test for $500 could save your brand.

- **Create a break-glass plan:** If someone hijacks your DNS, how fast can you recover? Do you know who to call? What about lost registrar access? Data recovery?

- **Phish yourself:** Don't know how? There are no-cost/low-cost phishing platforms and even browser-based tools to create safe tests described in Chapter 12 under "Individual". No malware. Just education.

Security testing for your side hustle is like insurance for your reputation, it only feels expensive until something breaks.

Quick Win for Side-Hustlers:

Task	Why It Matters	Tool/How-To
Website scan + recovery dry-run	Prevent cheap hacks and speed recovery	Mozilla Observatory, Sucuri, bug bounty options

The Mid-Cap Boss

"We run vulnerability scans monthly, that's enough, right?"

Nope.

Vulnerability scanners find issues.

Pen tests tell you what's exploitable. Not every "critical" vulnerability can lead to an exploitation, and not every "medium" is benign.

Red teams tell you what's compromisable, or already compromised...and no one noticed.

Maturity Levers That Matter:

- **Conduct annual pen tests...internal and external.** Don't just check the box...scope it for your entire attack surface. Read the findings. Fix them. Confirm they stay fixed (drift is real).

- **Run tabletop exercises with chaos:** What happens if finance gets hit with ransomware? What if a dev commits secrets to GitHub?

- **Build a purple team process:** When red-teams work hand-in-hand with defenders to improve detection, the results are powerful. Red finds, blue detects or tunes.

- **Test your backups, escalation paths, and IR procedures.** If you haven't fully tested it, it's a hope and a prayer, not a backup.
- **Red team your humans:** Try pretexting your own employees (ethically) or simulating social engineering attacks.

If your first red team exercise exposes glaring issues, good. Now fix them. That's the point.

Quick Win for Mid-Cap Bosses:

Task	Why It Matters	Tool/How-To
Pen tests + chaos table-tops annually	Exposes real gaps before attackers do	Nessus, Burp, in-house purple teams

The Enterprise Executive

"We pen test annually for compliance."

That's adorable.

Compliance isn't resilience. Nor is it security.

Real testing hurts.

It breaks things.

It reveals embarrassing truths about your **entire** IT footprint.

If your pen tests are clean every year, either:

- You have the best security team on Earth (nope).
- Or your pen testers are pulling punches.

Governance That Makes Testing Matter:

- **Executive-level red team briefings:** Not just technical findings—show business impact. "This exploit = access to payroll data" hits harder than "unauthenticated RCE."
- **Metrics that matter:**
    - Scope of the pen test... did it cover your entire attack surface, or was it just your PCI ***CDE***?

    - % of red team objectives accomplished
    - Mean time to detect during exercise
    - Mean time to remediate

- **Live-fire tests with real stakes:** No more sanitized environments. If it's not painful, it's not honest. Even better—schedule them without advance notice. If your SOC can't tell the difference between an exercise and a real attack... maybe it *is* a real attack.
- **Cross-org buy-in:** Legal, HR, PR, Ops—all should know what a simulated breach looks like. Tell the red team to pwn HR and watch the fireworks.
- **Third-party involvement:** If vendors have critical access, include them in your red teaming scenarios... of course, make sure your team clears across leadership and legal.

Quick Win for Enterprise Execs:

Task	Why It Matters	Tool/How-To
Real-world red team exercises with exec reporting	Turns "we're compliant" into "we're resilient"	Internal + external red teams, purple team reviews, legal tabletop

Real-World Fails

- **The "We Passed the Pen Test" Breach:** A company proudly cited its clean annual pen test...which had excluded cloud services, internal apps, and third-party integrations. Six months later, attackers came in through an exposed dev server with hardcoded credentials...something the test never touched. The breach exposed 12 million customer records. Turns out, you can't secure what you don't test.

- **The "Simulated Phish" That Was Real:** A red team sent a phishing email that mirrored a real attacker's recent campaign. It got clicked. No big deal, until the team realized the click led to a *live* malicious domain that wasn't part of the red team's infrastructure. Oops. The good news? The response plan kicked in and mitigated quickly. The bad news? It proved how vulnerable they were to the *real* thing.

- **The "Uncontacted Vendor" Failure:** A vendor with backend access to a healthcare portal was breached. Their credentials were used to access sensitive PII and billing records. The healthcare company had never tested vendor incident communication... and the delay in escalation added days to response, compounded regulatory exposure, and resulted in a seven-figure fine.

Final Thought for Chapter 16

You don't build muscle by thinking about working out.

And you don't build security by assuming your controls work.

You test. You probe. You break your own stuff.

Because when attackers do it first, the cost isn't just financial...it's reputational, operational, and potentially existential.

Whether it's a side project or a national defense system, the same rule applies:

Hope is not a control.

If you want to know whether you're truly secure, you have to prove it. Regularly. Relentlessly. And with ruthless honesty.

Quick Wins by Persona

Persona	Quick Win	Why It Matters	Tool/How-To
Individual	Audit your router, test backups, check breaches	Turns assumptions into visibility	Router UI, HaveIBeenPwned, iCloud/Drive backup test
Side-Hustler	Scan your site + simulate phishing	Hardens your brand and data against common attacks	WPScan, Mozilla Observatory, self-run phishing test
Mid-Cap Boss	Run a pen test + tabletop IR exercise	Identifies real-world exposure and sharpens response	Local consulting firm + internal response team
Enterprise Exec	Demand metrics + cross-org red team engagement	Makes tests meaningful, not checkbox theater	Red team briefings, SIEM integration, exec IR simulation

Chapter Seventeen

Training, IR... Slight Return

CIS Controls 14 & 17—Training and Response

Alternate Title:

Train Like You Fight, Fight Like You Train

Opening Story: "Training Is Useless If No One Believes It Matters"

In the aftermath of Uber's 2016 breach, two things became abundantly clear:

First, the breach wasn't just a technical failure...it was a **culture failure**. And second, the damage didn't stop at reputational bruises. It led to a **federal indictment**.

Let's rewind:

Attackers accessed a private GitHub repository used by Uber developers. What did they find inside? Credentials.

Those creds led directly into Uber's AWS environment, where the attackers found backups containing data on 57 million users and drivers.

Why were hardcoded credentials in a repo?
Why wasn't access gated?
Why didn't secure code reviews catch this?

All fair questions.
But the **real** question is:

Why didn't anyone sound the alarm before it became a national scandal?

Because security wasn't valued.
Because secure coding was just compliance noise.
Because "training" was a checkbox, and **nobody believed it mattered**.

When it came time to respond?
The leadership didn't disclose.
They paid off the attackers.
They tried to bury the breach under the rug.

The result?

- Uber's CSO was convicted, the first U.S. exec criminally charged for mishandling a breach.
- Uber paid $148 million in settlements.
- Public trust tanked.

And the worst part?

Most of the root causes were **already known risks**.
Training, policies, and reviews **existed,** but weren't **respected** or **enforced**.

And it's exactly why CIS Control 17 doesn't just say "do training." It says, **own the program. Drive the results. And align it to actual risk.**

Because if your people are "trained" (but still doing dumb things) it's not their fault. It's yours.

BLUF (Bottom Line Up Front)

Training programs don't stop breaches.

Trained, empowered people do.

CIS Controls 14 and 17 exist because human behavior isn't just a side quest...it's the battlefield.

But here's the rub:

- If your training is a checkbox, your users will treat it like one.
- If your culture doesn't reinforce it, you're just acting.
- If security isn't embedded into daily habits, it won't matter when it counts.
- If you don't train through the entire attack lifecycle, from Phish to Ransom note, to recovery, you aren't training.

Uber had training.

They had policies.

They had awareness decks.

But they didn't have a security mindset, and they paid the price.

Let's beat this drum a little harder across every persona.

The Individual

"Nobody ever taught me this stuff... it's daunting."

Most people don't want to do the wrong thing.

They just don't know what "right" looks like.

And that's why it sounds daunting. And that's why I wrote this book (and stood up the website). I want you to know what "right" looks like. It's not daunting when you have the information and instructions.

Security training isn't just for professionals. It's for anyone who uses a device, an account, or a network.

What You Should Learn (and Practice):

- **Recognize phishing and scams:** Learn the red flags: Urgency, sketchy URLs, unexpected attachments. Don't click, don't call the number, don't panic.

- **Stop oversharing:** Don't post personal data that can be used to guess passwords, security questions, or gain your trust.

- **Use a password manager** and MFA (you've heard this a lot by now... because it matters. A lot).

- **Talk about security** with friends, family, kids. You're more likely to remember and reinforce good behavior if you teach it to someone else.

- **Report incidents:** Don't shrug off weird pop-ups, unexpected password resets, or strange emails. Tell someone, or at least investigate. At a minimum, it's a good signal to reset your most important account passwords.

Security isn't your job title. But it is your job.

Quick Win for Individuals:

Task	Why It Matters	Tool/How-To
Basic scam spotting skills + MFA	Slashes common attack success rates	Free courses (Google Security Checkup, Cyber Aware)

The Side-Hustler

"I'm the whole company. I don't have time for security drills."

Exactly.

That's why **you** are the #1 target, and your #1 defense.

If you suck at cybersecurity long enough, you won't need to worry about having a company.

Take in all that stuff in the "individual" persona above and add in a few details for your growing business empire. Nobody *has* time for anything. They make time.

What You Need To Know:

- **Social engineering is aimed at you**, the solo operator. You're easy to spoof, scare, or persuade, and you have valuables.

- **Train your VA, your part-time developer, your social media manager.** If they touch your tools, they can cause harm. Your helpers can either be assets or liabilities. Train them to be assets. Remember, if your VA uses their own Gmail to access your systems, you've just added their hygiene to your threat model.

- **Set up process-based defenses:** Require voice confirmation for financial changes. Use templated email language so any deviation feels off. Set up processes and procedures that you follow... religiously.

- **Know how to respond to an incident:** If your Shopify store gets hijacked, do you know how to notify customers? Change your DNS? Revoke tokens? What about if your phone gets SIM-swapped? Map out how you'll recover so you can act fast when it happens.

Small business owners often get crushed not because they weren't aware...but because they didn't practice.

Quick Win for Side-Hustlers:

Task	Why It Matters	Tool/How-To
Incident playbook + VA training	Faster, calmer, cheaper response	Written checklist, secure contacts backup

The Mid-Cap Boss

"We do annual training and phishing tests. Done, right?"

Nope.

If you're checking a box instead of shifting behavior, you're not done. At best, you're **delaying** your breach headline.

Let's ask the hard questions:

- Is the training role-specific?
- Is it updated to reflect current threats (QR code phishing, MFA fatigue, ChatGPT-enabled scams)?
- Do people remember it after they leave the room (or the training module)?
- Does anyone measure how it impacts actual behavior?
- Do you have fully documented work-flows for any given compromise? Run books are a thing.

Maturity Levers That Actually Work:

- **Segment training:** HR, finance, marketing, and engineering face different threats. Teach and train accordingly.

- **Run phishing simulations, and celebrate the wins:** Make catching phish a badge of honor, not a gotcha. Farm your employees for ideas and input...you'll be surprised how much good they can do.

- **Use incident postmortems as training refreshers:** If a user clicked something bad, use it as a story (anonymized if needed). Stories stick. Your runbooks should be built from real incidents too, not hypothetical checklists.

- **Track metrics that matter:** Reporting rate, response time, escalation paths. Not just "did they click?" but "did they do the right thing after?"

- **Create feedback loops:** Let employees submit suspected phish. As suggested previously, build an "Is this sketchy?" Teams/Slack channel. Normalize curiosity, because those conversations are exactly what you want to solicit.

Training isn't an event. It's a behavior reinforcement system.

Quick Win for Mid-Cap Bosses:

Task	Why It Matters	Tool/How-To
Phish reporting channel + storytelling postmortems	Turns users into human sensors	Gophish, KnowBe4, custom Slack integration

The Enterprise Executive

"Our click rates are low. We're fine."

Cool story.

Ask Uber how that worked out.

Of course, Uber also had a leadership team that hid a breach, users who weren't empowered, and a culture that didn't value the security team's voice. You can definitely do better... let's get into how.

Governance That Embeds Awareness:

- **Make security culture a leadership priority:** If it's not in the executive performance plan, it's not going to show up anywhere else.

- **Hold leaders accountable:** Require execs to participate in training and phishing simulations. No exceptions. When breaches hit headlines, reporters don't ask about your metrics. They ask why no one spoke up...and who covered it up.

- **Use threat modeling to inform training:** If your biggest risk is BEC, your training should focus heavily on financial process hygiene and fraud recognition. If it's ransomware, focus on credential theft, intrusion detection, threat hunting, and immutable backup and recovery.

- **Tie training to incident response:** If someone fails a phish test, show them how it would've escalated, and what they could've done differently. Build runbooks to match the simulations. Take it all the way to the right of the equation...where the ransom note shows up on everyone's screens. It's not shaming, it's education and improvement.

- **Push training requirements down to vendors and partners:** If they have access to your systems or data, they should show proof of *real* training *and* retention...more than a PDF with a checkbox.

Security culture is a leadership function. If your teams don't care, it's because they haven't seen you care.

Quick Win for Enterprise Execs:

Task	Why It Matters	Tool/How-To
Leadership-level phishing tests + threat-based refreshers	Secures the last-mile human firewall	Targeted phishing campaigns, board-level reporting

Real-World Fails

- **The "We Passed the Audit" Breach:** A manufacturing company passed their SOC 2 Type I with flying colors. Six months later, a new employee clicked a phish that led to credential theft, unauthorized wire transfers, and weeks of recovery. Why? Their annual training never covered business email compromise, or what to do *after* clicking.

- **The "Executive Exemption" Mistake:** An executive exempt from phishing tests fell for a spoofed legal notice. His Office365 account was used to send internal emails laced with malware. It took two days and over 20 compromised inboxes before anyone caught it...because no one wanted to question the boss.

- **The "Untrained Contractor" Chaos:** A freelance web dev reused credentials between client projects. When their GitHub got breached, dozens of client API keys, including Stripe and AWS credentials, were exposed. Only one client had a security clause in the contract. The rest had to deal with the fallout alone.

- **The "Nobody Reports Anything" Org:** A regional healthcare org had decent security tools but no reporting culture. One staffer noticed odd MFA prompts...but ignored them. The attacker was already in, pivoting laterally for days. No one spoke up until patient data was being leaked. Silence is golden...from the attacker's perspective.

Final Thought for Chapter 17

Training is a fire drill for your brain.

If you don't make it real, regular, and tied to what people actually face. Then when the alarm sounds, they'll freeze instead of fight.

Train for chaos.
Test for failure.
Prepare for stupid.

Because when the breach happens, the winners aren't the ones with the best quiz scores.

They're the ones who already practiced saving themselves.

You can buy tools.
You can draft policies.
You can even pass audits.

But if your users don't **understand** what's dangerous, don't **believe** security matters, or don't **feel safe reporting** what they see...your program is a house of cards waiting for the next breeze.

Training isn't just "awareness."
It's behavior change.

It's cultural reinforcement.

It's battle drills.

And like all good drills, the point isn't to memorize answers.

The point is to *prepare for impact*...and bounce back stronger.

Train like you fight.

Because you fight like you train.

And if your users win a round against the bad guys? Celebrate it. Loudly.

They didn't just follow a policy, they protected your org.

Quick Wins by Persona

Persona	Quick Win	Why It Matters	Tool/How-To
Individual	Learn to recognize and report phish	Prevent account takeovers and fraud	Google security checkup, phishing test sites
Side-Hustler	Train contractors on basic threats	VAs and freelancers are your extended attack surface	Use free training from CISA, Google, Microsoft
Mid-Cap Boss	Segment + simulate	Tailored training builds muscle memory across departments	KnowBe4, Gophish, Microsoft Attack Simulator
Enterprise Exec	Embed security in leadership KPIs	Culture follows attention—if it's not tracked, it's ignored	Tie metrics to performance reviews and IR stats

Chapter Eighteen

Resilience

CIS Control 11—Data Recovery & CIS Control 17—Incident Response

Alternate Title: The One Where You Get Pwned, and Still Win

Opening Story: "So You Got Pwned. Now What?"

The SOC analyst stated frankly. "We've got someone running a scan from inside our network."

The CISO took a breath... "What do we know about it?"

"It's coming from one of our retail centers, and it's trying to connect to about 1500 machines simultaneously."

"Can you kill it?"

"No, it's not a managed device, but we are in the process of killing all the connections from the endpoints, and isolating that center. It should be off the network shortly."

30 minutes later, the CISO's phone was buzzing incessantly with texts (some included photos of their screens) from regional managers stating their machines had a message indicating their machines were locked up by ransomware. *Shortly* wasn't fast enough. Why? About half the regional managers had not shut down their machines to apply a patch, and were vulnerable to this zero day.

After seeing the first of the screenshots, the CISO jumped on the phone. Then he turned to the analyst. "I've called our IR retainer, the war room is standing up now. Is our ***WORM*** backup with our golden images still accessible?"

"Yes, and we'll start shipping new laptops immediately. The regional managers should be back up and running in a couple of days."

The next two weeks were spent with the IR team going through every inch of the network, cleansing it of the invader's footprints and ensuring no backdoors were left. As for the rouge ***CCTV*** camera that caused it all? The building owner was indifferent... it hadn't cost him anything.

Inevitably, someone is going to breach your defenses and land inside your perimeter. And you're going to think through it all:

You did all the things.

You patched.

You trained your people.

You locked down your cloud.

You phish-tested your CEO (and somehow lived).

And still (somehow) attackers got in.

It happens.

Because no matter how good you are, **perfect prevention is a fairy tale**.

The real pros?

They plan for failure.

They design for pain.

They build systems, processes, and mental muscles that bend instead of break.

This chapter isn't about keeping bad things from happening.

It's about making doubly sure they **don't kill you when they do**.

BLUF (Bottom Line Up Front)

Even after you do everything right, you can still get wrecked.

Resilience is about:

- Rapid detection
- Effective containment
- Confident recovery
- Surviving the bad day—and coming out swinging

Cyber resilience isn't just for enterprises.

It applies to individuals, hustlers, and mid-caps just as much.

It's not about **if** bad stuff happens.

It's about **how** you recover, rebuild, and rebound.

And here's the hard truth:

- If your backups weren't tested, they don't exist.
- If your processes aren't documented, they won't be followed.
- If your response depends on perfect conditions, it'll collapse

under pressure.

Let's break it down by persona.

The Individual

"They hacked my email. I'm ruined!"

Nope...not if you planned ahead.

Remember all that stuff we've covered in the previous chapters? That's going to pay off now. This isn't a bedtime story, it's the world we live in now. And ignoring it is going to hurt worse than doing what I'm suggesting here.

Let's get rolling.

Your Resilience Playbook (when something goes wrong):

- **Refer to your written personal incident response plan (that you created because you've been reading this book):** Keep a document with all major accounts, phone numbers, backup codes, and account recovery steps for each. Make sure you have information for filling out IRS (form 14039), contacting the FTC (identitytheft.gov), and local law enforcement if needed.

- **Reset accounts in priority order:** You should have set up an account recovery process for all important accounts. Email (including your backup email you set up after reading this book) and Phone first (they are the root), then financial, then everything else. Change your Social Security password (yes, that's a thing), and report fraud.

- **Enable MFA everywhere (this should have been done before, but better now than never):** Especially on anything you just had to reset. Prefer app-based or hardware MFA, not SMS (especially if they took over your old phone number).
- **Use identity theft protection tools:** If you didn't have it set up before, set up an account immediately... Some banks offer it for free. If not, consider LifeLock, Aura, or even Credit Karma's alerts.
- **Backups:** Check your backups, and recover from them if needed. They're in a reputable cloud back up, encrypted, and tested, right?
- **Lock it down:** Know how to freeze your credit with Equifax, Experian, and TransUnion. Do that immediately if you suspect your email, phone, or other critical account has been compromised. Ideally this has been frozen since you read this book.
- **Bonus move:** Before you get hit, create an encrypted archive of this info and store it offline (USB, printed copy in a fire safe, etc.).

Quick Win for Individuals:

Task	Why It Matters	Tool/How-To
Backup + recovery codes	Saves your digital life when it all burns	Google, iCloud, physical 2FA keys

The Side-Hustler

"My site got hacked. Am I done?"

Well...

Your Shopify store is redirecting to a crypto scam.

Your Stripe account got locked.

Your Gmail inbox is full of complaints—and you don't even have access.

You're done... Only if you didn't prepare.

Your Resilience Playbook (include everything in the Individual section):

- **Backups, backups, backups:**
    - Weekly database dumps into a trusted back up service (Carbonite, iDrive, Acronis, etc. Don't just set up a ***NAS (Network Attached Storage)*** and back up to that... they'll own that in seconds)
    - Static copies of your site into that same service
    - Off-platform customer list backups (same services, but choose encrypted!)
- **Break-glass access plan:**

    - Secondary admin account (on a separate domain or email service)
    - Auth app on a second device or paper backup codes
- **Define your recovery chain:**
    - How do you regain control of DNS?
    - Who do you contact if your payment processor locks you out?
- **Incident templates:**
    - Email to customers
    - Post for social channels
    - Message for payment partners
- **Lock down third-party tools:**
    - Rotate API keys (this should be happening regularly anyway)
    - Ensure least privilege on all integrations is in place

Quick Win for Side-Hustlers:

Task	Why It Matters	Tool/How-To
Website + DNS backup plan	Restores your storefront, fast	Local database dumps, registrar login audits

The Mid-Cap Boss

"We got hit with ransomware. The CEO is asking if we have options... do we?"

Only if you practiced before it mattered.

Your Resilience Playbook:

- **Restore from your backups:** This should be straight-forward now, because you've been testing your restores monthly, right? You know how many of your systems are locked up. You've simulated partial and full recoveries. And, you tracked time to completion and logged errors. Now you can give the CEO an estimate of when you'll be back up.

- **Because you've used immutable backups/WORM storage:** You're able to tell the CEO that you'll only lose the differential between now and the last backup for your production DBs, VMs, and key application data. He's not happy that things went south, but he's happy you have a handle on it and real answers.

- **Confirm the status of all your dependencies:** Because you documented your dependency chain, including what apps, services, and credentials that each system rely on, you can verify that those are live and ready to go. And, you created system runbooks that cover all of them.

- **Bring your warm standby environments up to production:** You pre-staged your cloud infrastructure or data center infrastructure to be ready in minutes, not days. Your CEO fought you on this, because it had an on-going overhead cost that didn't project directly to top-line revenue. But now he's glad you stood firm.

- **Measure how you're doing against your defined Recovery Point Objectives/Recovery Time Objectives per system:**

    - ***RPO = Max data loss you can tolerate***

    - ***RTO = Max downtime you can tolerate***

As you bring systems back online, report up-chain to leadership how you're doing. If you had all of the above set up, you're probably killing it. Champion your teams that made it possible.

- **Because you simulated ransomware scenarios, everyone is on board:** Remember when we wanted you to include comms, legal, finance, IT, and execs in the table top exercises? That's paying off now.

- **Communicate:** All those communication templates we discussed? Those are paying off, as you literally hand them to the CEO and the corp comms teams, and you get back to work.

Quick Win for Mid-Cap Bosses:

Task	Why It Matters	Tool/How-To
Immutable backups + ransomware runbook	Buy time when everything else is burning	AWS S3 Object Lock, Veeam, Rubrik

The Enterprise Executive

"Our stock is tanking. Regulators are calling. What now?"

This is where leadership shines...or gets wrecked.

You've read all of the above. You know enough just from that, but let's ask a few questions.

Does Your Resilience Playbook:

- **Set resilience as a strategic priority?** Is it built on cyber risk frameworks and board-level ***OKR***s? Is it budgeted to your ***risk tolerance***?

- **Leverage tiered BC/DR planning?** Critical apps should have near-zero RTOs. Non-critical systems can wait.

- **Implement multi-tiered backups?** Hot (instant), warm (same-day), and cold (offline, air-gapped).

- **Require SBOM + rebuild pipeline for key systems?** Have you ensured you can recompile/redeploy any compromised app.\?

- **Adopt chaos engineering practices?** Do you run failure simulations (Gremlin, LitmusChaos) in non-prod to test recovery?

- **Formalize cloud-specific recovery plans?**
  - AWS: Use S3 Versioning + Object Lock, AMI snapshots, cross-region replication.
  - Azure: Use Recovery Services Vault, Geo-Redundant Storage.
  - GCP: Leverage Snapshots + Cloud Functions for recovery automation.
- **Define post-breach governance process?**
  - Root cause analysis with public findings (when possible)
  - Re-certification of impacted systems
  - Retrospective funding discussions tied to actual risk
- **Include a Crisis Communications Playbook?** Do you have draft press releases, regulatory notification letters, customer FAQs prepared?
- **Address Insurance?** Do you know your cyber insurance terms *cold*? (Spoiler: notifying the wrong party or making unauthorized payments might void coverage.)
- **Include Legal Playbooks?** Do you have ready-to-go breach notification templates for GDPR, CCPA, SEC, HIPAA, and state laws?
- **Define Board Briefing Procedures?** During crisis mode, leadership needs concise, confident updates. No technical jargon. Just impact, recovery, timeline.

Quick Win for Enterprise Execs:

Task	Why It Matters	Tool/How-To
Crisis comms plan + legal templates	Stops PR disaster and fines avalanche	External counsel review, PR agency on retainer

Real-World Fails

- A small eComm site hosted on WordPress was hit with ransomware. The backups? On the same server. Encrypted. Gone.
- A healthcare org discovered that their cold backups had never been tested, and restores failed due to corrupted images. They lost six weeks of patient data.
- A mid-cap manufacturer didn't realize their domain registrar was tied to a single exec's Gmail account. When it got hijacked, they lost access to DNS, email, and their website.
- A global enterprise who got hit with ransomware first tried to restore production from their Dev environment. Problem? Dev was a month behind. Then they paid the ransom, and the keys were corrupted and didn't decrypt the files. The 30 day gap cost $11M in lost transactions and SLA violations on top of the six-figure ransom.

Final Thought for Chapter 18

You can't win every battle.

But you can plan to survive every one of them.

Resilience isn't sexy.

It's not glamorous.

It doesn't get splashy headlines.

But it's the difference between **crisis** and **comeback**.

Quick Wins by Persona

Persona	Quick Win	Why It Matters	Tool/How-To
Individual	Freeze credit + recovery cheat sheet	Stops downstream identity fraud	FTC IdentityTheft.gov, password manager
Side-Hustler	Create break-glass access plan	Regains control when creds get popped	Use secondary email + MFA backup codes
Mid-Cap Boss	Test restore process monthly	Most backups fail at recovery, not creation	Spin up test restores + document results
Enterprise Exec	Fund immutable storage + simulate failover	Shows you're serious about bouncing back fast	AWS S3 Object Lock, DR drills w/ full staff

Chapter Nineteen

Level Up—Learn, Grow, Hack Yourself Better

CIS Control: All of Them

Alternate Title:

"Because Knowing Is Half the Battle"

Opening Thought: You've Come This Far. Now What?

You've read the rants. You've seen the war stories. You've probably questioned a few of your own life choices by now (like realizing that all of your passwords have the same root of "PapaSmurf"?).

But awareness isn't the finish line. It's the starting gate.

This chapter isn't a lecture. It's a map. A curated, non-boring set of resources to help you actually build the skills, habits, and confidence to put everything in this book into action.

Whether you're a digital newbie, a side-hustle warrior, a mid-cap decision-maker, or a CEO of a 52-country behemoth...there's a next step for you.

Let's go find it.

The Individual

"Where do I even start?"

"Where do I even start?"

Right here. You don't need a CompSci degree or a rack of certs to start locking down your digital life.

Learn It

- Cybersecurity & InfrastructureSecurity Agency (CISA) Tips. Read this frequently. (https://www.cisa.gov)

- Have I BeenPwned? Check to see if your credentials are showing up on the darkweb. (https://haveibeenpwned.com)

- Mozilla Privacy Not Included: Reviews gadgets for security/privacy (https://foundation.mozilla.org/en/privacynotincluded/)

- Stop. Think. Connect Toolkit (https://www.stopthinkconnect.org/)

And visit this books website to learn specifics on the topics covered here, as well as new information...the bad guys never stop evolving, so we need to do the same.

Do It

- Download a password manager: Bitwarden, 1Password
- Set up MFA on your accounts: Start with email, banking, cloud storage
- Use a DNS filtering app like NextDNS or Quad9 for safer browsing
- Check your credit reports for free at AnnualCreditReport.com
- Lock your credit down, and only open it when you need a loan

Gamify It

- Try a phishing quizzes: Do it quarterly, set a reminder in your calendar. (https://phishingquiz.withgoogle.com/)
- Use a "cyber hygiene" checklist* quarterly. Yes, also make this a calendar event.

The Side-Hustler

"I'm one person with a dream... and an overloaded inbox."

"I'm one person with a dream... and an overloaded inbox."

Exactly why security matters.

Learn It

- FTC's Cybersecurity for Small Business (https://www.ftc.gov/business-guidance/small-businesses/cybersecurity)
- OWASP Top 10 (https://owasp.org/www-project-application-security-curriculum/)
- Google's Cybersecurity Starter Guide (yes, it's solid) https://www.cloudskillsboost.google/paths/419/course_templates/966/video/469581
- UpGuard's Data Breach Archive: Learn from others' mistakes (https://www.upguard.com/breaches)

Do It

- Use Stripe or Square to handle payments (use their iFrame, don't store credit card data)

- Enable logging and backups on your site or store
- Set up cloud backups for everything: Google Drive, Dropbox, etc.
- Install security plug-ins if using WordPress: Wordfence, iThemes Security

Test It

- Run Mozilla Observatory (https://observatory.mozilla.org)and OWASP ZAP (https://www.zaproxy.org/) against your domain
- Set up a free Gophish instance to simulate phishing for your team/VA (https://getgophish.com/)

The Mid-Cap Boss

"Security is on our roadmap... somewhere."

"Security is on our roadmap... somewhere."

Yeah, we noticed.

Learn It

- NIST Cybersecurity Framework (https://www.nist.gov/cyberframework): Not as painful as it sounds
- CIS Controls v8 (https://www.cisecurity.org/controls/v8): Free, readable, actionable. It's what this whole book was framed on.
- Microsoft Learn Security Tracks (https://learn.microsoft.com/en-us/training/paths/)
- SansSecurity Cyber Aces (https://www.sans.org/cyberaces/)

Build It

- Use Rumble or Axonius to get visibility
- Get a ticketing system: Freshdesk, Jira, or even ServiceNow if you've got the budget

- Use KnowBe4 or Wizer for awareness training
- Mandate quarterly patch reviews and risk assessments

Measure It

- % of assets with owner + patch status
- Time from phishing click to escalation
- % of employees reporting suspicious activity

The Enterprise Executive

"We're working toward a Zero Trust transformation with continuous control validation across a hybrid architecture."

Cool. But have you read your own security policies? You're in charge of an Enterprise.

Let's get schooled up to that level:

Read This

- CISA's Zero Trust Maturity Model (https://www.cisa.gov/zero-trust-maturity-model)
- MITRE ATT&CK Framework (https://attack.mitre.org/)
- CIS Risk Assessment Method (CIS RAM) https://www.cisecurity.org/insights/white-papers/cis-ram-risk-assessment-method
- Maestro Threat Modeling for AI Systems (https://maestro.ai): If you're touching AI, this matters

Ask These Questions

- Are our KPIs tied to business outcomes or audit reports?

- Can I see dashboards from our TVM, CMDB, and SIEM in real time?
- Do we test our vendors' training and incident response?
- Is cybersecurity represented in M&A, product launches, and board planning?

Fund It

- Purple team exercises
- Threat modeling training for architects and product managers
- Security architecture reviews baked into SDLC
- Dedicated GRC analyst to track and report control efficacy

Final Thought for Chapter 19

Cybersecurity isn't something you finish. It's something you get better at.

Start where you are. Use what you have. Learn what you need.

No matter your persona, whether you're securing your mom's Netflix password or managing the blast radius of a global zero-day, there's always a next step.

This chapter gave you resources. The rest is on you.

Go build. Go break. Go level up.

Chapter Twenty

Conclusion: The Only Way Out Is Through

So here we are.

You've read stories of BEC scams and skull-and-crossbones screen takeovers. You've learned about rogue routers, forgotten servers, CEO voice deepfakes, sketchy browser extensions, and the black hole that is your untracked asset inventory.

You've walked through every CIS Control in context of your persona, from knowing what you've got to making sure someone's actually watching when it breaks. Along the way, we broke down what security *actually* looks like for:

- You, the **Individual**, trying not to get phished by your printer.
- You, the **Side-Hustler**, balancing e-commerce dreams with API keys and plug-in hell.
- You, the **Mid-Cap Leader**, pretending your asset spreadsheet is a strategy.
- You, the **Enterprise Executive**, wielding the influence to change

everything... or wreck it.

And now?

Now you've got a roadmap. A battle-tested, field-informed, no-BS blueprint for how to *not* suck at cybersecurity.

Let's call out what matters most.

1. Cybersecurity is a Culture Problem...Disguised as a Tech Problem

It's tempting to believe that if you just buy the right tools, check the right boxes, and pass the annual audit, you're safe.

You're not.

Tools don't protect you. *People using tools correctly* protect you. And that means behavior, accountability, and reinforcement...over, and over, and over again.

Every incident in this book, real or inspired by real-world events, happened because someone didn't:

- See it
- Say something
- Do something

Training and awareness aren't side quests. They're the main game.

2. You're Already in the Fight...Even if You Didn't Sign Up

Whether you're a small Etsy seller, an accountant with a smartphone, or a Fortune 500 CEO...if you use digital systems, *you're a target.*

That's not fear-mongering. That's math.

And if you think, "no one would bother with me," remember: **Attackers aren't targeting you. They're targeting everyone. At scale. With automation.**

They don't have to know your name. They just have to find the port you left open. Or the password you reused. Or the email you forwarded without thinking.

3. Defense Scales with Discipline, Not Budget

Yes, bigger companies have more resources. But they also have more legacy systems. More politics. More people clicking "Remind Me Tomorrow."

Small organizations have speed, flexibility, and focus.

You don't need a seven-figure budget to get security right; you need to do the *right* things, consistently. And that starts with inventory, patching, training, access control, monitoring, and culture.

The basics are hard because they're relentless. But they work.

4. You Don't Have to Do Everything...Just the Next Right Thing

Look, nobody masters all 18 CIS Controls overnight.

Nobody implements Zero Trust in a quarter. (And if your vendor says otherwise, throw them into the river.)

But *you can start*:

- With a home Wi-Fi scan
- With a list of your cloud assets
- With one policy that actually gets read

- With one phishing test that gets reported
- With one incident response checklist that's printed, posted, and practiced

Security isn't an all-or-nothing game. It's cumulative. Iterative. Built one "not today, attacker" decision at a time.

5. You're the Hero of This Story

You, reading this book.

You are the last line of defense between your systems and someone else's payday.

And that's not meant to freak you out. It's to **empower you**.

Because now, you know more than most. You've seen what failure looks like. And you've got the tools to fix it...wherever you are in your journey.

Whether you're protecting your email account or your company's entire global infrastructure...

Whether you're fighting budget apathy in the boardroom or click-happy chaos in your family group chat...

Whether you've got 50 users, 5,000 endpoints, or just 5 minutes a week to focus on cyber...

You've got a path forward now.

And here's the final truth:

Cybersecurity isn't about perfection. It's about momentum. And the best day to start was yesterday. The next best day is right now.

So go do the thing.

Patch the box. Print the plan. Write the policy. Train the people. Fix the mess.

You've got this.

Let's go.

— *Vince*

Glossary

777

A Unix file permission setting that grants read, write, and execute permissions to everyone (owner, group, others). Basically, your application becomes Lady Godiva sporting a mohawk... full exposure.

Access Control

The methods and policies used to limit who can view, use, or modify resources... basically rules and tools that say "you shall not pass"...unless you're on the list. Think nightclub bouncer, but for files and servers.

Actuators

The tiny robots behind the curtain. They take digital commands and turn them into real-world actions: Like opening valves, moving arms, or launching missiles (hopefully not yours).

Ad Blocker

Your browser's bouncer for shady marketing. Also blocks malware masquerading as "one weird trick to lose belly fat."

API (Application Programming Interface)

These rules, protocols, and tools act as an awkward translator between two pieces of software... think two rhinos trying to work together without a shared love language.

API Keys

Secret codes your app uses to say, "Hey, I'm allowed in here!" Treat them like passwords. Sadly, people don't.

Asset Inventory

A list of all the tech you own, use, or forgot was plugged in behind the vending machine. If you don't know what you have, neither will your firewall.

Attack Surface

Every possible way an attacker could get in. Think of your digital life as a house...every window, door, doggy door, and chimney counts.

Authentication

The process of proving you are who you say you are. Not to be confused with "trust," which takes longer and usually requires bringing donuts.

Auto-Updates

When your software patches itself without asking. Magical. Until it breaks something critical five minutes before a board meeting... but still keep it enabled.

Automated Infrastructure

Your servers now build and deploy themselves like overcaffeinated interns. Just don't forget who gave them that power.

AWS (Amazon Web Services)

Jeff Bezos' galaxy-sized public cloud playground where your entire business probably lives, even if you're not sure how it got there. If not here, it's in Google Cloud, Microsoft Azure Cloud, or any one of the myriad other clouds that make up the global storm of "someone else's servers".

Bandwidth

How much data you can shove through your internet pipe. Kind of like water pressure, but for cat videos and corporate VPNs.

BEC (Business Email Compromise)

A scam where cybercrooks trick your team into sending them cash, creds, or gift cards. Usually involves an urgent-sounding email from "the CEO" to send something, or a vendor request to change a bank transfer destination...neither is valid.

Bot

An automated script that does things fast...sometimes helpful, sometimes evil, always relentless.

Botnet

A zombie horde of hacked devices doing the attacker's bidding. You might even be part of one if you visit sketchy websites or open random links. You don't need to be in cybersecurity to be in a horror movie.

Bitcoin

Digital gold mined by Graphic Processing Units (GPUs) and marketed by libertarians and scammy YouTube influencers. The go-to payment for ransomware gangs.

Breach Corpuses

Mass graves of leaked usernames, passwords, and secrets. Hackers love 'em. Odds are strong you show up in a few.

Browser

The app you use to get to the rest of the internet. Also: the front door to 90% of phishing attacks.

Browser Extensions

Tiny add-ons that do cool stuff like translate pages, block ads, or secretly spy on you. Choose wisely.

Browser Session Tokens

Your digital hall pass. Keeps you logged in while you surf. But if it gets stolen, the hacker gets your pass...and probably your data.

Bug

A software mistake. Some bugs are harmless. Others delete your thesis and torch your bank account.

Bug Bounty

A modern gladiator pit where hackers find flaws in your software...for cash. Cheaper than a breach, and way more fun for both of you. HackerOne and BugCrowd are two good services.

Cache

Your computer's digital junk drawer. Speeds things up... until it doesn't.

CCPA (California Consumer Protection Act)

The California law that tells companies "You can't just hoard people's data like it's Pokémon cards."

CCTV (Closed Circuit Television)

Security cameras that watch everything and can launch malware or massive Distributed Denial of Service (DDoS) attacks... unless they're unplugged.

CDE (Cardholder Data Environment)

Everything that touches, stores, or transmits credit card data. Basically, the stuff every criminal would love to own, and makes CISO's twitchy.

CIRT (Computer Incident Response Team)

The team you pray is caffeinated and available when the fan starts spinning and throwing chunks of breach all over your data center.

CIS (Center for Internet Security)

The nonprofit nerds who make hardening guides and set security benchmarks that no one reads or enforces until after the ransomware hits... and then it's generally too late to care.

CIS Benchmarks

Step-by-step instructions to configure your systems securely...aka the IKEA manuals of cybersecurity, but less Swedish. And still people try it without reading the instructions.

CISO (Chief Information Security Officer)

The poor soul tasked with securing your entire digital empire while herding cats (analysts), dodging executive politics, and explaining (again) why just copying data to another drive is not "backup."

Client Isolation

The practice of putting your devices in digital time-out so they can't gossip across the network. Especially useful when you don't trust your smart fridge or your kid's malware-infested tablet.

Cloud

Someone else's computer. Really. That's all it is. Just with a fancier invoice.

CMS (Content Management System)

A magical black box that lets non-tech folks build websites (and attackers inject malware) with equal ease. See also: WordPress plugin roulette.

Cookies

Tiny files websites leave behind to remember you. Not nearly as delicious as the name implies.

Configuration Hygiene

The digital version of flossing. Boring, often skipped, but absolutely necessary if you want to avoid decay... and disaster.

Containers

Little shipping crates for code. Portable, fast, and insecure if you forget that the contents still need locks, alarms, and fire extinguishers.

Continuous Assessment

Because "set it and forget it" only works for rotisserie chickens, not cybersecurity programs.

Credential Stuffing

When bad guys take your reused "Fluffy123" password and try it across the internet like it's a skeleton key to your whole life. Spoiler: it often is.

CRM (Customer Resource Management)

A system that keeps track of your customers so you can forget to secure their data at scale. A hacker's buffet if misconfigured.

Crypto

A digital currency revolution, or the fastest way to lose your life savings and explain to your spouse why your "investment" turned into a meme.

Cryptography

Math magic that turns your secrets into gibberish, unless you're careless, in which case it turns your gibberish into breached data.

CSPM (Cloud Security Posture Management)

Tools that exist to remind you that cloud security isn't automatic, and that your misconfigured S3 bucket has been public for six months.

CSVs (Comma Separated Values)

Spreadsheet grenades. Easy to open, easy to share, and often holding data so sensitive it should come with a warning label.

CVEs (Common Vulnerabilities and Exposures)

The giant, ever-growing to-do list of everything broken in tech. Like a shopping list for hackers.

CVSS (Common Vulnerability Scoring System)

Because we needed a numeric way to argue whether a vulnerability is "bad" or just "meh, we'll patch it later."

Dashboards

Where security teams pretend to be pilots, staring at a hundred blinking lights and hoping none of them crash the business today.

DAST (Dynamic Application Security Testing)

Poking a live app with sticks to see if it leaks secrets, explodes, or politely hands over your customer database. (Spoiler: it usually leaks.)

Data Classification

The corporate art of figuring out whether the spreadsheet you emailed to "All Staff" included PII, trade secrets, or just lunch orders.

Data Leaks

When your data pulls a Houdini and escapes into the wild. Bonus points if no one notices until it hits the news.

Data Sprawl

The digital equivalent of hoarding. If you've got 42 copies of last year's budget scattered across laptops, USBs, and cloud drives, you're doing it wrong.

Data-Aware Policies

Security rules that take context into account, because not all data is created equal, and some of it really shouldn't be emailed as an attachment named "FinalFINALv3_reallyFINAL.xlsx."

Digital Go Bag

A prepper's kit for the cyber age: backups, passwords, and emergency plans. Because when disaster strikes, Google Docs won't save you if Google's down.

DKIM (DomainKeys Identified Mail)

An email signature that proves you didn't spoof yourself. (Or that the phisher at least tried hard enough to forge it convincingly.)

DLP (Data Loss Prevention)

That system that tries to stop users from emailing the company's crown jewels to their cousin's Hotmail—assuming it doesn't just block everything useful instead.

DMARC (Domain-based Message Authentication, Reporting and Conformance)

Your email domain's bouncer. Keeps the impersonators out, but only if you set it up properly...and most don't.

DMZ (Demilitarized Zone)

A network buffer zone where services go to be accessible... and occasionally sacrificed to the gods of public exposure.

DNS filtering

A technique that blocks access to certain websites or content by filtering Domain Name System queries like a digital bouncer at the club entrance...if a domain's not on the list, it's not getting in. No shoes, no shirt, no SSL? No service.

Drive-by Download

Malware that hops on your system just because you visited a sketchy site. Like picking up lice at a gas station.

EDR (Endpoint Detection and Response)

Security solutions that monitor, detect, and respond to threats on endpoints. Think a security camera with a taser for every laptop and server...if something sketchy shows up, it's not just watching, it's throwing punches.

Encryption

Your data's invisibility cloak using complex math and voodoo. Unless you hand the attacker the keys by accident.

Endpoints

Devices such as computers, mobile phones, and servers that connect to a network. Basically, every digital doorknob that can open your house to hackers—including that cool smart-toaster. If it blinks and connects, it's a target.

ESL (English as a Second Language)

English is notoriously difficult for non-native speakers to master despite it being the native tongue of 95% of error messages, ambiguous documentation, and keyboard-smash variable names.

Exfiltrated

Data that has been illicitly transferred out of an organization. The classy word for "someone jacked your files and bolted."

FBI's IC3 (Internet Crime Complaint Center)

A center for reporting internet-related criminal complaints to the FBI. It's where your phishy tales should go after you've been duped; a digital confessional that note taking meets federal note taking.

File/Field level encrypted

Encryption applied to individual files or specific fields within a database. The difference between locking your whole house vs. putting a padlock on your sock drawer. Fine-grained paranoia.

Financial Verification

Processes used to confirm the legitimacy of financial transactions or accounts. Trust, but verify, especially when Jeff in Accounts suddenly wants to wire $200K to Nigeria.

Firmware

Software burned into hardware devices. Barely updateable code that lives in your hardware rent-free and can serve as launchpads for malware.

FIDO2 (Fast Identity Online 2)

A set of standards for passwordless authentication using public key cryptography. FIDO2 finally asks, "What if we just got rid of passwords entirely?" Spoiler: Implementation is king here...screw it up, and it's a free-for-all for the criminals.

Firewall

A security device or software that filters incoming and outgoing network traffic. The doorman with attitude; it lets the regulars in, but drop one shady packet and you're on the curb.

Fraud controls

Measures and processes put in place to detect and prevent fraudulent activities...because sometimes "Bob from Finance" is actually Vlad from somewhere cold, and he's really interested in your wire transfer process.

GDPR (General Data Protection Regulation)

The EU privacy law that resulted from one Belgian dude's quixotic battle against giant tech. The reason every website now has a cookie pop-up and your marketing team cries a little every day.

GitHub

A web-based platform for code version control and collaboration using Git. Like Dropbox for code...except public by default and often full of secrets people forgot they left in there.

GLBA (Gramm-Leach-Bliley Act)

A US law requiring financial institutions to explain information-sharing practices and protect sensitive data. The "you must tell me what you're doing with my money stuff" law that banks love to ignore until audited.

Gold images

Pre-configured, secure system images used as templates for deploying new systems. The cyber equivalent of cloning your cleanest kitchen, before the toddlers and malware move in.

Governance

The framework of policies, processes, and controls ensuring security objectives are met. Fancy talk for "who's actually steering this ship, and are they sober?"

HaveIBeenPwned

A public service that allows users to check if their accounts were exposed in known data breaches. The depressing website that confirms, yes, your password from 2008 is now public knowledge.

Hard Drive

Computer hardware that holds and spins a magnetic or optical disk and reads and writes information on it.. now largely a solid-state affair where your digital life lives. Also known as "the thing that dies unexpectedly right before a big presentation."

HIPAA (Health Insurance Portability and Accountability Act)

A US health data law whose tenets have yet to be maturely implemented by any healthcare entity. The rulebook that says "please don't leave patient records on a Post-it, Karen."

HMI (Human-Machine Interface)

The user interface that connects an operator to the controller for an industrial system. Where meatbags push buttons to tell robots what to do...and sometimes what to explode.

HVAC (Heating, Ventilation, and Air Conditioning)

Your building's lungs, and like real lungs, if compromised, everything else starts to fail (including your security).

Hardened container templates

Pre-configured container images with enhanced security settings. Docker, but with fewer gaping holes. Because "default" settings are hacker catnip.

IAM (Identity and Access Management)

Frameworks and technologies for managing digital identities and access to resources. The bouncer, guest list, and velvet rope all rolled into one. No ID, no access.

ICS (Integrated Control System)

Systems integrating various control mechanisms, often used in industrial environments. Where robots talk to other robots and humans mostly just cross their fingers.

IdP (Identity Provider)

A service that authenticates users for Single Sign On and other access models. The digital gatekeeper that says, "Yes, that's who they say they are. Probably."

IDS (Intrustion Detection System)

Monitors network traffic for suspicious activity. Throws a tantrum when something doesn't look right, but doesn't stop anything from happening.

IP Address

Your computer's home address on the internet. Think of it as the return address attackers use when they want to pay you an unsolicited visit.

IP vs. MAC Address

IP = Internet address. MAC = Hardware name tag. One changes, the other doesn't...unless you're a hacker and changing them is tradecraft.

IPS (Intrusion Prevention System)

Monitors network traffic for suspicious behavior, and then immediately karate-chops anything that looks suspicious. Basically, IDS with a taser.

IMAP/POP

Email delivery protocols that date back to when floppy disks were cool. Still running your inbox like it's 1997? This is why attachments still break.

Immutable Backup

A backup that can't be altered: Kind of like the opinions you formed in college, but useful in a ransomware crisis.

IRP (Incident Recovery Plan)

Your company's official plan to pretend it was totally ready when everything catches fire. Spoiler: most haven't updated this since that one tabletop in 2019.

IR (Incident Response)

The process and team that shows up after the breach and tries to figure out how bad it really is. Think digital paramedics, with more caffeine and less sleep.

ISPs

The people who sell you internet access and then throttle it when you need it most. Also useful for blaming when you don't want to admit your Wi-Fi password is "admin123".

IaC (Infrastructure as Code)

Turning servers and networks into code so devs can break prod faster and more efficiently than ever before.

IoT (Internet of Things)

Your doorbell is connected to the internet and talks to your fridge which talks to your toaster. None of them are patched. This is why your vacuum is mining crypto.

Just Enough Access (JEA)

The security version of "don't touch that, it's not yours." Grants exactly what's needed and not one byte more.

Kill Chain

A fancy term for "how attackers go from knocking on the door to robbing your house." Defenders use it to implement controls while attackers use it to break in.

Latency

The delay between asking and receiving based on how much overhead the developers baked into the processes. Think of it as the "awkward pause" of the internet.

Least Privilege

Give users just enough access to do their job...no more. Especially Dave from Marketing, who somehow keeps requesting domain admin rights.

Local Admin

That powerful account on your machine that holds god-like powers, and that malware *loves*. It's like giving burglars the keys to your house *and* your Netflix login.

MFA (Multi-Factor Authentication)

The use of two or more of the three authentication factors: Something you

Know, Something you Have, and Something you Are. Because passwords alone are about as secure as locking your front door but leaving the key under the mat labeled "KEY."

MFA Recovery Codes

The one-time codes for when your MFA goes south... you definitely saved them somewhere "safe" and now can't find. Hope you didn't lose your phone too.

MTTD (Mean Time to Detect)

How long it takes you to notice the bad guys are already inside. Faster is better. Days is bad. Months is breach-notification letter bad.

MTTR (Mean Time to Respond)

How long you flail before plugging the hole the bad-guys found. Bonus points if you don't make it worse in the process.

Metasploit module

The defacto plug-and-play tool for pen testers and bad guys alike. It's like Ikea for hacking: insert part, click button, exploit assembled.

NAS (Network Attached Storage)

A file-level computer data storage server connected to a computer network providing data access. Your file-sharing treasure chest, and likely the most neglected, unpatched device on your network. Please update it. Please.

NDR (Network Detection and Response)

A collection of people, processes, and technologies that make up the part of your security stack that watches the traffic and yells "that's weird" and kills suspect processes when your thermostat pings Russia.

NFT (Non-Fungible Token)

A digital receipt proving you "own" a JPEG image of a gorilla. Mostly used for art, flexing, or losing money in new and exciting ways.

NIST (National Institute of Standards and Technology)

The U.S. agency that writes more security standards than you'll ever have time to read...but you're expected to comply with all of them.

NSA (National Security Agency)

Where the phrase "we're from the government and we're here to help" gets very encrypted, very fast. Also your default boogeyman.

OAuth

A secure protocol that enables you to log in with another service by exchanging a secure token. Convenient until that one gets popped and brings the whole tower of tokens crashing down.

OKR (Objectives and Key Results)

A framework for pretending you're aligned with business goals, right before everyone ignores it until Q4 panic sets in.

Open-Source Software

Software whose source code is publicly available for inspection and modification. In theory, "secure" because thousands of strangers are squinting at your code and alerting you (maybe) to issues... basically you're hoping someone nice finds the bug first.

Operating System (OS)

The boss-software of your computer upon which all other applications depend. Windows, macOS, Linux...pick your poison.

Out-of-Band

Communication or data transfer that occurs outside of the primary communication channel. For when you're yelling into a walkie-talkie because Slack just got popped.

OWASP ZAP

Open Web Application Security Project Zed Attack Proxy; a tool for finding vulnerabilities in web applications. Think of it as a browser's mean older sibling who finds every weak spot in your site and points at it while laughing.

P1 finding

A critical or highest-priority issue found during a security assessment. Translation: Drop everything. This is the security equivalent of your kitchen being on fire.

Password Manager

A software application that helps users store and manage their passwords securely. Because "Fluffy123!" shouldn't unlock your bank account, your email, and your kids' daycare photos.

PAM (Privileged Access Management)

Tools and processes for managing privileged accounts and access. Basically, a babysitter for your most powerful user accounts...because they can't be trusted to behave.

Patch

A software update designed to fix vulnerabilities or bugs. It's like duct tape for your app, only with more rebooting and less redneck engineering. Apply them unless you like bleeding data.

Patch Lag

The time between a fix being released and you actually installing it. The gap where attackers make their millions, and you sob with regret.

Patch Management

The process of applying updates to software and systems to fix vulnerabilities. Also known as "The Thing We Forgot to Do Right Before the Ransomware Hit."

Patch Tuesday

The day Microsoft releases new patches, and hackers read them like a treasure map. Please patch on Tuesday.

Payload

The part of malware that does the dirty work...the rest is just the carrier pigeon. Kind of like the sharp end of a cyber-spear.

PCI (Payment Card Industry)

The Payment Card Industry Data Security Standard (PCI-DSS) is a set of rules that says, "If you want to take cards for payment and not get fined into oblivion, follow these."

PDF (Portable Document Format)

Arguably the most popular file format for internet documents. Loved by HR, hated by security teams, and occasionally weaponized by cybercriminals. It's the mullet of file formats: business up front, mayhem in the back.

Penetration Test (Pen Test)

A simulated cyberattack against your systems to test defenses. Hackers with permission slips. They break in, take notes, give you a report, and ideally don't leave surprises behind.

Phishing

A cyberattack that uses disguised emails or messages to trick people into revealing sensitive information. When that "urgent email from the CEO" is actually Vlad in his basement asking for gift cards.

Phishing vs. Spear Phishing

Phishing: mass scam. Spear phishing: custom scam just for you. Both suck. One sucks worse.

PHP

A popular server-side scripting language for web development. Infamously flexible, and often responsible for some of the internet's most regrettable security holes.

PHP shell

A script written in PHP that provides a command-line shell interface to a web server, often used by attackers to set up shop on your systems. Congratulations, your server is now someone else's playground. Hope you didn't leave anything important on there.

PII (Personally Identifiable Information)

Information that can identify an individual, such as name, address, or social security number. The stuff that gets stolen, leaked, sold, and reused more than your Netflix password.

Ping

A polite digital "Are you there?" Used for testing. Or for nerds trying to sound cool: "I'll ping you later about our next cyber conference".

PIPL (Personal Information Protection Law)

A Chinese data privacy law regulating personal information processing. China's way of saying "we care about your data..." Interpret that how you wish.

PITR (Point-in-Time Recovery)

Restoring systems to a specific moment before an incident. Because sometimes the only way forward is to go back to yesterday and pretend today never happened.

Playbook

A documented set of procedures for responding to specific security incidents or scenarios. A "when not if" manual. Like fire drills, but with more encryption and fewer smoke detectors.

Plugins

Software components that add specific features to an existing computer program. Tiny add-ons that can either make your app sing...or scream in agony when compromised.

Port (Networking)

One of 65535 communication endpoints that allows different applications or services to send and receive data over a network. Basically, a digital doorway on a device. If it's open, stuff gets in. If it's left open unintentionally...welcome to HackerTown.

POS (Point-of-Sale)

Systems where retail transactions are completed. Also, the literal point where you realize your store's Wi-Fi password is "password123" and now someone just bought a flatscreen with your inventory system.

PAM (Privileged Access Management)

Tools and processes for managing and monitoring accounts with elevated access rights. Because giving everyone admin rights and "hoping for the best" is not a strategy.

RAM (Random Access Memory)

Computer memory that temporarily stores data and machine code currently in use...i.e. stuff it's working on right now. Think: short-term memory. Or that thing your browser eats every time you open one more tab.

Ransomware

Malware that encrypts a victim's files and demands payment for the decryption key. The digital equivalent of waking up to find your office tied to railroad tracks. Pay up, or else. Not as big an issue if you have Immutable Backups.

RCA (Root Cause Analysis)

A method of identifying the underlying causes of a problem or incident. The post-breach autopsy. Spoiler: It's almost always user error or a patch someone "forgot."

RDP (Remote Desktop Protocol)

A protocol for remotely connecting to and controlling another computer. Fantastic for IT support. Even more fantastic for attackers when left open to the internet with no password.

Red Team

A group that simulates real-world attacks to test an organization's security defenses. They break in, steal your secrets, then politely hand them back and invoice you for the trauma. Think hired hackers paid to break into your systems just to prove your security sucks, so you can't pretend it doesn't.

Ris

The chance that something will go catastrophically wrong, usually because someone said, "It's probably fine." Business try in vain to quantify this...see Risk Evaluation.

Risk Evaluation

A formal process of realizing, "Wait, this could really mess us up," and assigning a number to how bad that mess would be.

Risk Tolerance

The amount of chaos your organization is willing to live with before someone in a suit finally notices. At the board level, it's "how much money can we lose and still make a profit."

Role-Based Access

Giving people only the access they need based on their role, not the access they want, because your intern shouldn't have root.

Root

A superuser account on a computer or network and has complete control. Root owns everything, and a hacker with root owns you.

Router

A computer and networking device that forwards data packets between computer networks. The magical box that makes your internet work, until someone unplugs it to charge their phone.

Router vs. Modem

Modem talks to the internet. A router talks to your devices. Confusing them is like yelling at your microwave when the oven isn't working.

RPO (Recovery Point Objective)

The amount of data you're willing to lose before someone throws a chair. Hint: If your answer is "none," you're lying.

RTO (Recovery Time Objective)

The maximum time your systems can be down before your customers riot and you start panic-buying backup generators and whiteboards.

S3 Bucket

Amazon's object storage through a web service interface...in other words their data virtual dumpster, where your secrets go to be accidentally left public for the world to find.

SaaS (Software-as-a-Service)

The subscription model where you rent software monthly forever... because owning things is so 2005.

SAM (Software Asset Management)

The practice of keeping track of your software licenses so you don't get a "friendly" letter from Adobe with a six-figure fine attached.

Sandboxing

The digital playpen where you put sketchy stuff so it doesn't trash your real systems...hopefully.

SAST (Static Application Security Testing)

Like spellcheck for your code, except it's hunting for vulnerabilities that could bankrupt you. If you build code and don't have this...the end is near.

SBOM (Software Bill of Materials)

The ingredients label for your codebase which often includes a number of question marks...so you know if your app is 90% open-source duct tape and dreams.

SCADA (Supervisory Control and Data Acquisition)

The systems quietly providing automation that runs power grids and water plants...on Windows XP...over the public internet. Most cyber folks wake in cold-sweats when dreaming of these.

Scripts

Tiny bits of code that automate tasks, break things in milliseconds, or both...depending on your luck.

SDK (Software Development Kit)

A boxed lunch for developers: pre-packed tools to build software faster, but with bonus compatibility drama, and occasional baked-in vulns.

SDLC (Software Development LifeCycle)

The seven-stage journey of building software: from "great idea" to "legacy nightmare no one wants to touch."

SEC (Securities and Exchange Commission)

The government body that doesn't care about your zero-days or how your business survives the attack...just your failure to report them fast enough.

Security Awareness Training

The corporate version of sex-ed: boring, awkward, and occasionally life-saving if anyone pays attention.

Segments (i.e., Network Segments)

Digital walls between your crown jewels and your smart coffee maker. Without them, that server in Mexico can talk to your production plant in Detroit. If you're not using them, why even bother?

SEO (Search Engine Optimization)

The dark art of convincing Google you're not irrelevant. Sometimes used by legit marketers, often by snake oil salesmen and paid spammers.

Session Hijacking

You establish a session once you've authenticated to a web application.

Then the attacker steps in, kicks you out of your own digital house, sits in your chair, and orders pizza using your account.

Shadow IT

Everything your employees install without telling IT. Also known as "how breaches happen for free."

Shell Code

Malicious little bundles of doom that give attackers a place to launch remote control of your system, because your app forgot to sanitize input.

Shodan

A search engine for the Internet of Things...or, in hacker-speak, "Google for stuff people forgot they left wide open." Want to find exposed webcams or unprotected industrial systems? Shodan's got you.

SIEM (Security Information and Event Management)

Where logs go to die...or to alert you at 3 a.m. because someone mistyped a password. Think of it as the brainstem of your Security Operations Center, if your brainstem needed constant tuning and a $400k subscription.

Skeleton Key

A sneaky bit of malware that lets attackers log in as anyone they want. It's like giving someone the master key to your hotel...only the hotel is your Active Directory, and you're now bankrupt.

SLAs (Service Level Agreements)

Contracts full of promises that vendors *definitely* won't meet, but will tell you they did, because "99.9% uptime" includes every outage that didn't make the news.

SOAR (Security Orchestration, Automation, and Response)

A collection of software programs developed to bolster an organization's cybersecurity posture. AKA: Automate all your bad decisions faster. If your alerts are junk, congrats...you've just made junk alerts run at scale.

SOC (Security Operations Center)

A room full of blinking screens, caffeine, and overworked analysts begging for threat intel that actually makes sense. It's where cyber dreams go to get triaged, ticketed, and sometimes (if you're lucky) resolved.

Social Engineering

The art of getting someone to hand over the keys to the kingdom...by just asking nicely. Phishing, pretexting, tailgating...basically hacking humans, which is easier than hacking tech.

SPF (Sender Policy Framework)

An email security standard that tells the world which servers are allowed to send email on your behalf. Of course, it's optional, confusing, and half the internet ignores it. Good luck!

SSH (Secure Shell)

Secure Shell. AKA: The "remote in and fix it at 2 a.m." protocol. Secure...unless you forget to turn off password auth or leave "root" enabled with "toor" as the password.

SSO (Single Sign On)

Login once, access everything. The dream for users. The jackpot for attackers who phish that one login. It's like having a master key...let's hope you don't lose it.

Supply Chain Attack

Why hack you when I can hack your underpaid vendor who forgot to patch their Jenkins box? If you trust the people you outsource to, you'd better also verify...*everything*.

TCP (Transmission Control Protocol)

The protocol that ensures your cat videos arrive in perfect order. Reliable, chatty, and often abused by attackers who enjoy the same reliability when exfiltrating your data.

Test

That thing you *meant* to do before pushing code to prod. In security, "test" often means throwing attacks at a system and hoping nothing breaks too loudly.

Test Ports

Ports you open "just temporarily" and forget to close for six months. They're the breadcrumbs attackers follow when you leave your digital picnic unattended.

Threat Modeling

Sitting down to imagine how the bad guys might wreck your stuff—before they actually do. Basically cyber Dungeons & Dragons, but with more regulatory pressure and fewer dragons.

Ticketing

The bureaucratic paper trail for every fire you're putting out. If it's not ticketed, it didn't happen. Bonus points if your ticketing system has more bugs than your production code.

Tickets

Tiny units of hope that someone, somewhere, will fix your problem. Spoiler: It's probably you, and it's after hours.

Time-bound elevation

Temporary admin access... assuming you remember to turn it off. Because nothing screams "least privilege" like full root access until someone forgets they had it.

Token theft

When your authentication tokens get stolen, and now someone halfway across the world is you...but evil. Pro tip: Tokens are like car keys...don't leave them lying around unencrypted.

TLS (Transport Layer Security)

The technology that keeps your credit card safe while buying novelty socks online. Unless you're still using TLS 1.0, in which case...good luck, friend.

Tor (The Onion Router)

The underground railroad of the internet. Great for whistleblowers, journalists...and criminals selling fake passports for Bitcoin. Anonymity: with extra levels of sketch.

Trojan

Malware that shows up pretending to be something useful (like a PDF resume) then wrecks your network. History's original bait-and-switch scam, now in executable form.

Trusted Context

Where everything behaves like it's supposed to...until someone abuses trust and nukes your audit logs. "Trust, but verify" should really be "Don't trust, and verify constantly."

UPnP (Universal Plug and Play)

A helpful protocol that automatically opens firewall holes...because who needs control or security when your smart TV wants to talk to the toaster?

Unpatched

A polite way of saying "waiting to be hacked." You *know* the fix is available. You just haven't gotten around to it...yet. Neither has half the internet.

Unsupported. Fully privileged

A system with admin rights, no updates, and zero vendor support. Basically, it's the cybersecurity version of driving a flaming car with no brakes, and no insurance.

Visibility

Your ability to see what's going on in your environment before attackers do. If your idea of "visibility" is a monthly Excel report, you're legally blind in cyber terms.

VLANs (Virtual Local Area Networks)

Your network's attempt at social distancing...segments that keep devices from getting too cozy. Great in theory, ignored in practice.

VM (Virtual Machine)

A pretend computer running inside a real one. Handy for testing, isolating risky stuff...and sometimes accidentally exposing prod to the sandbox.

VPN (Virtual Private Network)

Your digital invisibility cloak that wraps your data in an encrypted tunnel... Doesn't make you anonymous, just slightly harder to follow home. Encrypts your traffic, until your users tunnel Netflix through it and melt your bandwidth.

Volume Encrypted

Your entire disk is locked down with encryption. Nice. Just don't lose the key, or your backups become a modern art piece titled "Lost Forever." Oh, and when your using any data on that disk, the entire disk is no longer locked down.

Vulnerability Management

The never-ending whack-a-mole game of finding and fixing flaws before someone else does. Think "to-do list from hell" but with CVEs and compliance audits.

Vulnerability Scanner

Your security bloodhound...except it sniffs out old software instead of drugs. Just remember: It finds stuff. *You* still have to fix it.

WAF (Web Application Firewall)

Yet another bouncer, but this time for your website: blocking sketchy requests, but occasionally turning away legit users for wearing the wrong digital shoes.

Windows Server 2000

A digital fossil of a server OS still running somewhere because "it just works." Which is true...right up until it works for the ransomware gang too.

WORM (Write Once, Read Many)

Unchangeable storage. Great for backups, audit logs, and proving that yes, Steve did click that phish, again.

WPS (Wi-Fi Protected Setup)

A "security" feature so bad it should've come with a "Do Not Use" sticker. Push-button pairing for people who hate passwords and love risk.

Wi-Fi

Wireless networking. Convenient for you, *very* convenient for attackers parked outside your house with a Pringles can antenna.

WordPress plugin

A chunk of code you add to your website without reading the reviews. Sometimes helpful. Sometimes malware in a friendly costume.

ZTNA (Zero Trust Network Access)

Trust nothing. Verify everything. Especially the intern with "temporary" admin rights and a curiosity streak a mile wide.

Zero-Day

A bug so fresh, nobody's patched it yet...not even the vendor. Attackers love them. Defenders dread them. You? Just hope it's not in your stack.

Acknowledgments

Nobody is an island—least of all me.

My career has been built on the backs of mentors, colleagues, employees, friends, and family. I can't possibly list everyone who's shaped my journey, but a few deserve special mention:

- **Jeff Boonmee,** my first technology mentor, who taught me that growth and curiosity aren't optional...they're the job.

- **Richard Whitlock**, who championed our "Wizards" cyber warfare cell in the 101st and whose calm, caustic snark inspired my own.

- **Jeff Crane**, my alter ego in risk-taking, who showed me it's okay to tank, as long as you come back stronger.

- **Craig Olsen, Paul Kipping, and Taylor Wilson**, the kind of security colleagues you wish you could always work with and somehow occasionally get to do just that.

- **Morian Eberhard**, who taught me what it looks like to be truly engaged, "all in," and unflinching when others fall short.

And most importantly:

- **My family:** Who has endured more than I can describe so that I could chase this career across continents, crisis calls, and countless missed family events.

- **My conviction in Christ**. Regardless of your faith or lack thereof, it's impossible to argue that if the world aligned to the principles taught by Him in the Beatitudes, this book would be unnecessary.

Lastly, to everyone out there who's clicked the wrong thing...and learned from it:
You give me hope that we might just win this war after all.

About the Author

Vincent Romney has spent more than two decades fighting on the front lines of cybersecurity, across battlefields, boardrooms, and break rooms. With over 22 years of combined Active-Duty, Reserve, and Air National Guard service in Information Systems, Information Operations, and Cyber Warfare, he's seen the cyber fight from both the military and civilian sides...and spoiler: it's a mess on both fronts.

In the private sector, Vincent has served as Head of Cybersecurity and CISO for companies ranging from $80 million startups to $2.7 billion multinationals operating across 52 countries. He's helped secure complex global infrastructures, survived regulatory audits without losing his mind (mostly), and led teams through ransomware attacks, nation-state aggressors, and everything in between.

Through it all, one thing became crystal clear: cybersecurity isn't just a technical problem. It's a human one. And most people, through no fault of their own, were never taught how not to suck at it.

This book is the answer he wishes he'd had to hand to family, friends, side-hustlers, small business owners, and even the C-Suite when they said, "What do I really need to know about security?"

When he's not building security programs or speaking at conferences, Vincent is probably somewhere off-grid: Skiing, climbing, racing, or scheming his next book. Because if there's one thing he's learned, it's that the fight never ends.

Appendix

CIS Top 18 Critical Controls: (reprinted with permission from the CIS)

If you're diggin' what I'm puttin' down here...here's a list of things that may just push you into the deep end.

Introduction to IT & Cyber Security (Cybrary): https://www.cybrary.it/course/introduction-to-it-and-cybersecurity

Cybersecurity training courses: https://www.udemy.com/topic/cyber-security/

Gandalf CTF Range: https://gandalf.lakera.ai/do-not-tell

AI Guardrails & Responsible AI: https://www.endtrace.com/responsible-ai-course-beginners/

DevSecOps Essentials (DSE) (EC-Council): www.eccouncil.org/cybersecurity-exchange/cyber-novice/free-cybersecurity-courses-beginners/

Introduction to Cybersecurity (Cisco Networking Academy): https://www.netacad.com/courses/introduction-to-cybersecurity

Secure Coding Online Training Course (Cybrary): https://www.cybrary.it/course/secure-coding

Application Security & Web App Hardening: https://www.udemy.com/topic/cyber-security/

AI Red Teaming, Prompt Hacking, & AI Security Masterclass: https://learnprompting.org/on-demand-masterclass

LLM Guardrails: https://arize.com/blog-course/llm-guardrails-types-of-guards/

Made in the USA
Monee, IL
13 September 2026

62981861R00203